Wounded Healing

The Art and Soul of Surthriving

Jorja Jamison, PhD, LP

For more information, go to the author's website at

www.jorjajamison.com

Cover and interior design by David Ter-Avanesyan

Cover illustration by Justin Thomas

Jorja Jamison Counseling and Consulting, LLC

ISBN (paperback): 979-8-9910055-0-0

ISBN (e-book): 979-8-9910055-1-7

Library of Congress Control Number: 2024914449

Dedication

To Sarah, without whom this book, and my life, would not be possible.

and

To all the health care providers who specialize in treating addiction.

You are very special people.

Contents

Preface

The title of this book has profound significance for me. The concept of the *wounded healer* goes back millennia, first appearing in recorded history in Greek mythology.

Chiron was a centaur (part human, part horse) who was widely known as a great healer and teacher. An orphan, Chiron was raised by Apollo and taught the healing arts. He then took what he learned and brought it to humans, becoming a renowned mentor to many. His students included many of the great heroes of Greek mythology such as Jason, Achilles, Hercules, and Esculapius, known as the father of modern medicine. Chiron is credited with the creation of botany and pharmacy.

Though immortal, Chiron was hurt accidently by one of Hercules's poisoned arrows and suffered an incurable leg wound. No matter what Chiron did, he was unable to heal his own wound. Eventually he relinquished his immortality because of this insufferable pain. His story is told to emphasize the irony that one of the world's greatest healers couldn't heal himself.

This theme has echoed throughout medicine and other healing traditions. The idea that healers are wounded themselves—and that they practice medicine or give help as a displaced attempt to heal themselves—is highlighted in many cultures, from African shamanism to the story of Christ to the origin stories of many modern superheroes. In the 1950s, Carl Jung, a psychiatrist, coined the term "wounded healer" and pondered that perhaps the counselor's suffering was what served as their greatest teacher in working with wounded clients. He believed that the therapist's ability to care for the inner wounds of others depended on their own ability to closely access their inner wounds.

I first learned of this archetype in graduate school, in my last year of classes. The professor for my last clinical placement brought in a reading from Michael J. Mahoney's *Constructive Psychotherapy: Theory and Practice*. It was the final chapter of the book where Dr. Mahoney reflected on his own journey of becoming a psychologist and shared what it meant to be both human and a therapist. He recounted his unlikely career path and described his experiences as a wounded healer.

I read every word with eyes wide, devouring the book; I had never heard someone talk so vulnerably about self-doubt and the fragility of the psychologist's soul. Much of my own journey and being seemed to be reflected in his writing. I soon realized my theoretical orientation was highly aligned with his—to something called *constructivism*. I read his assertion that every therapy session changes the therapist at least as much as it changes the client. That had definitely been my experience during my clinical rotations. But what most impacted me was his comfort with being a wounded healer—that in fact, he found power in this. I had struggled for years in graduate school, wondering if I was too wounded to become a psychologist. Here, in one chapter, I was given permission to be wounded; nay, I could be celebrated for it. I still had a long way to go, but this was a key turning point for me.

I call this book *Wounded Healing* to note the active state required to do this work. The gerund *Healing* reflects that this is a doing, not a being.

We actively battle as we heal. And we are actively wounded even as we are actively healing others. It's the active process of engaging in our own healing that gives us the greatest abilities to help others.

The subtitle of this book, *The Art and Soul of Surthriving*, provides the path of this healing, from barely surviving to joyously thriving. The concept of *Surthriving* deeply applies to people in recovery from many of life's struggles—including grief, grave mental health conditions, and especially substance use disorders. Many people spend decades just barely surviving in their active addiction, yet their recovery allows them to reach a place of thriving. And as counselors, we use research and evidenced-based practices, to be sure, but there is an *Art* to our work—a creativity and openness. Above all else, wounded healing requires we do this work from the seat of our *Souls*.

I have also organized this book very intentionally. It includes Wounded chapters, where I share the chronological story of my wounds, and Healing chapters, where I share non-chronological lessons I've learned in my circuitous path of healing. I'm a fully licensed psychologist now, and a professor, so many of the Healing chapters include many of the concepts I teach my clients and students. I interweave the Wounded and Healing chapters to show that we often do this work in tandem. That even while being wounded, we are capable of healing others. This sometimes presents a jarring effect (to be ripped from a deeply painful chapter into one of hope and healing, only to be thrown back into suffering). This effect is intentional, and I think conveys the experiences of my life, where I was deeply wounded on the inside, but capable of providing much healing and hope to others on the outside. Readers may choose to read this book straight through to experience this effect themselves, or they may choose to read all the wounded or healing chapters together.

My hope is that this book helps others in their paths of healing, including counselors in training, people in recovery from substance use disorders, and anyone else who has struggled in life. The stories I tell in this book are my recollections, to the best of my ability. We've known in psychology for some time that memories are malleable, and that two people engaging in the same experience can have vastly different memories. Whenever possible, I back up my writing with outside sources such as medical records, journals, and police reports. However, it is possible that my memories differ from others who experienced things with me, and I acknowledge this. I attempt to deal with stories about any real people as sensitively as possible, recognizing that most people are just doing the best they can with what they have and where they are. I've also had others review this manuscript for accuracy; however, all mistakes remain my own.

And finally, a word about language: there is some controversy about how to refer to people who have problems with substance use. Often people are labeled as "addicts," or "alcoholics," and these labels confer a very negative stigma. Within the field of treatment, we are trying to help people use more person-first language such as "a person with a substance use disorder." This helps us see that there is a person underneath all that use, that a person is so much more than their troubles with substance use, and that what, in fact, they are dealing with is a mental disorder.

However, many people who have a substance use disorder still describe themselves with the term "addict" or "alcoholic," claiming it as an identity. I am one of those people. Therefore, in the book, you will see me use the term "addict" to identify myself; but usually, when I am referring to the clinical work I am doing, I use the term "people with substance use disorders." I encourage you to defer to the person-first term whenever referencing another person, while respecting that some people might use a different term to describe themselves.

Introduction

I don't know the exact moment I became an addict, but I know it happened by the time I was 5.

In preparation for kindergarten, the elementary school sent a list of supplies each parent was supposed to acquire, things like safety scissors, paste, crayons, and the like. I saw the word "tablets" on this list. Now, the school was talking about writing tablets, the pads of paper with the solid and dashed lines that students use to practice their letter writing. However, the only tablets I was aware of were tablets of medicine. I clearly remember tagging along on my mother's shopping trip, excited to buy these "tablets." I thought, *You get to take pills to go to school? How COOL!* I could feel an energy coursing through my body. This is how I know I had a special relationship with pills by the age of five.

When I was born, I was sick a lot. I was colicky and had a lot of breathing issues. The country doctor wisdom of the time advised my mother to leave me in my crib, so I would learn to self-soothe. For the first year of my life, the two primary times I was held were when I was getting fed or being given medicine. So it's no wonder that my two addictions became food and pills. This is where my story begins.

It would be nice if this was a story of a person who had an addiction, sought help, got cleaned up, and went on to get her doctorate in psychology in order to help others. But that is not my story. My addictions persisted for decades—through graduate school, through my internship, and into my professional career as an addiction psychologist working at one of the world's most prestigious treatment centers. This is the story of a woman whose entire personality was shame-based, and whose childhood wounds created an adult who was driven by perfection and invulnerability. This path is lined with years of deep depression, crippling social anxiety, and decades spent living as an imposter. It is a story of extreme isolation, of someone desperate for connection but incapable of intimacy. This is my story.

But this is also the story of how I was finally able to heal, with the help of some amazing people. This is the story of a journey to self-compassion, with detours down codependency lane and abusive relationship alley. This is a story of triumph, of coming face to face with my fundamental life force and making peace with the world. Along the way, I learned what it means to be a counselor, how to truly sit with someone in pain, and how to help others find their own path of healing. This is also my story.

Let us begin.

Wounded 1

Childhood

I grew up in a family that was unable to tolerate any form of intimacy.

I come by my addictions honestly; by this I mean I come from a long line of addicts. I once heard it said at an Alcoholics Anonymous meeting by another member that if you shook their family tree, empty whiskey bottles would fall out. That description would fit my family as well, although very few of my family members were aware of or would acknowledge their addictions. I later learned that Dr. Claudia Black, a specialist on addiction and codependency, lists the three rules of the alcoholic home as "Don't Talk, Don't Trust, and Don't Feel," and these three rules were strictly enforced in my family.

My one saving grace was that, for some reason, I was born with extraordinary intelligence. I excelled academically, and this allowed me a path out of my family home at age 15. I have absolutely no doubt that if I'd remained at home until I was 18, I would not be alive today.

Because of my academic prowess, I skipped seventh grade. I attended a small kindergarten-through-eighth-grade school in rural Eastern North Carolina. My entire eighth grade class consisted of 18 people.

I'm sure I was pretty full of myself at the time. Because of this, or for whatever reason, I experienced extreme social rejection from my new peers.

That entire year, I was relentlessly bullied. Ostracized. Books-thrown-in-the-trash-on-a-regular-basis, things-written-about-me-on-the-bathroom-wall, people-refusing-to-sit-near-me-during-lunch bullying. The only way I can describe it now is social trauma.

This was the year I first attempted suicide. I was 12 years old.

I can look back only in gratitude now that I attended school before the advent of social media; at least I was given a daily reprieve while at home every night. Had Facebook and Snapchat been available, I would have experienced this bullying 24-7.

At the same time, I had no safe person at home to seek solace from. I became deeply depressed. I wanted out of life. Several times throughout that spring, I would raid the medicine cabinets at home, take a handful of pills, and lay down in bed. I remember each time relaxing my body into the mattress, feeling a peaceful relief; the pain was about to be over. Each time, however, I did not die. I always woke up the next morning, realized my attempt was not successful, and recognized that I was going to have to get up and go back to that school that day. Words seem to fail in describing the despair I felt.

One suicide attempt was serious enough to land me in the hospital for two days. At thirteen, I had combined a few handfuls of pills with half a fifth of vodka, and began vomiting profusely early the next morning. My mother discovered me—and the empty pill and vodka bottles—and in a panic, raced me to the emergency room, which was an hour away.

Twenty years later, I obtained my medical records from this visit. I learned from these records that my mother first stopped at the office of our family pediatrician and tried to get him to see me privately without having to admit me to the hospital. I can only guess this was to keep my suicide attempt from becoming public.

I was lethargic and not very responsive. My temperature had dropped to 95 degrees, my heartrate was 140 beats a minute, and I could not stop vomiting. The pediatrician convinced my mother to take me to the ER where he admitted me to a general pediatric floor.

My mother communicated to me and everyone else afterward that I had been hospitalized due to "an adverse reaction to medication." I actually thought that she managed to have this recorded in my medical chart, but when I got the records later, the term *suicide attempt* is used throughout.

Once I got home, we never spoke about what actually happened with anyone, including each other. I didn't even have a conversation with my sisters about this event until we were all in our 20s.

In my psychiatric assessment report in my medical records, I listed my reasons for wanting to die as "not having friends, being overweight, and having low grades." I weighed 135 pounds. I verbalized that any grade below 97 was unacceptable. These were the levels of perfection I was already expecting of myself.

Looking back at the records and my memories of the event, I so clearly see a desperately depressed young woman. Both the hospital and my pediatrician recommended follow-up psychological care. My parents, not wanting me to see someone locally, arranged an assessment with a psychologist a few hours away. I fully participated in the cover-up, adamantly asserting that this was in no way a suicide attempt and I was fine. I made up a story that the ingestion of the pills and alcohol was due to a dare. After a couple of visits, I didn't have to see him anymore. And I didn't receive any further psychological help for several more years.

I can't blame my mother for her behavior. . . . She was under tremendous pressure to present our family as ideal. My father was a well-known attorney who had just been elected to the state senate. My mother didn't know how to help me, but she knew how to show up. And she also was the only one who did. Every single nursing note (and there were dozens) in my hospital record from the two days lists her as being at my bedside. I overheard her on the phone with my father at one point; he was several hours away at the state capital. She was begging him to come, not only to be with me, but to support her. I didn't hear the excuse he used, but I saw what it did to my mother. She looked crushed.

He never came, the entire two days I was in the hospital. He did, however, arrange for flowers and a box of chocolates to be sent. When these arrived, I joined my mother in feeling crushed.

Healing 1

The Imposter Syndrome

There's a common phenomenon called the imposter syndrome that often affects both people with substance use disorders and graduate students, so it's no wonder I got a double dose of it. It's talked about fairly regularly now in psychology and counseling programs, but when I was a student, I didn't hear about it until the end of my doctoral program.

My practicum supervisor told us one day that it's common for people in graduate school to feel like they're imposters. That they somehow got into graduate school by mistake, and sooner or later, the school would figure this out and ask them to leave.

I looked at the instructor incredulously as he said this. *How could he know this is exactly what I've been thinking for years?* I wondered. Coming from my background, as a student with no training in psychology prior to graduate school, I just *knew* the school was going to say at some point, "You know, we thought we'd give it a try—to admit a student with no training or background—but it's time to end this experiment. Clearly you're too far behind. We made a mistake."

As the instructor told us about this phenomenon, I looked around and saw the heads of other students nodding. *Wait, other people feel this way?* I asked myself.

Well, it turns out a lot of other people feel this way. It's also a common theme shared by speakers telling their stories in recovery meetings. Most of us with imposter syndrome feel at some point that we're somehow ill-equipped for life, like everyone else got an instruction booklet, but not us.

This feeling persisted for me despite any growing level of education or accomplishments. And this fear was greatly reinforced by my addiction.

The truth is, for 10 years, I *was* an imposter. I barely made it into graduate school, and I barely finished the program--it took me four years longer than most students. I went on to take a job as a mental health practitioner, and three years later I became a professor who trains counselors in a Master's program. During this whole time I presented as a confident, sober clinician and counselor educator, when in fact, I had a secret: I was getting high most days and doubted everything about myself. I was providing counseling to patients on how to recover, while my own personal life was a mess. I spoke at 12-step meetings about how to stay sober, when in reality, I had just swallowed another pill before coming into the building.

So for me, one of the greatest gifts of recovery is no longer feeling like an imposter. It was a long road to overcome this, and I'll share this journey throughout the book. What I feel inside, I'm now able to portray outside. I ended up staying with the job as professor, and it's where I still work today.

Imposter syndrome, although more widely acknowledged and discussed now, is still rampant. These days, I make it a point to talk to each incoming class at my school about the imposter syndrome during the first days of orientation. I describe the characteristics, and the common thought of graduate students that they are not supposed to be here. As I do, I look around the room at a group of wide-eyed students whose faces are awash with being found out. I recognize that look, and I smile and reassure them that they're in the right place.

Healing 2

Three Tasks

A lot has been made of something called the *therapeutic alliance* in therapy. This is the strength of the bond between counselor and client. In fact, in research the alliance has been found to be more important to therapeutic outcomes than whatever treatment the therapist actually uses.

Historically, the therapeutic alliance is defined as consisting of three parts: a warm emotional bond between client and counselor, a mutual agreement on the goals of therapy, and a mutual agreement on the tasks of therapy. Without these three ingredients, the client tends not to make progress. In fact, they might even dig in their heels and get worse.

I personally have found the therapeutic alliance is critical in all the work I've done, both as a counselor and as a client. I've had clients drop out of counseling because we didn't have a good bond, and I've fired my own therapist over disagreements on goals and tasks.

While the therapeutic alliance is seen as foundational, it does not describe what the counselor needs to *do* to be successful. I've come to believe that counseling comes down to doing three jobs: see, accept, and join.

First, my job is to *see* my client. All of the person. See them in the context of their environment and culture. See them and how they've been surviving. See what they are showing me and what they are keeping hidden. And see the parts of them they can't see themselves.

My second job is to fully *accept* the client. This is actually the hardest part. I define acceptance as letting go of *any* desire that the client be any different than exactly how they are. This is where I find most counseling students struggle. They want the client to participate in treatment a certain way, be completely motivated for change, or have the same goals as they do. They get upset when the clients don't do their homework, or don't take their suggestions for continuing care after residential treatment. I have found it is important that I get to a space where I don't *need* the client to change. The client is exactly where they are supposed to be. And this is what allows me to do my third job.

My third job is to partner with the client—*joining* them and helping them get to where *they* want to go. The destination must be determined by the client; otherwise, we're working on my agenda, not theirs. It is not until this step that we can talk about goals; without seeing and accepting, I can't really help someone get to where they want to go.

I'm often surprised at what the client identifies as a goal. Sometimes it's a fairly obvious external goal—like I want to get back my family, or I want to avoid jail—but sometimes clients surprise me. One client told me they wanted to stop feeling afraid all the time. Another told me they wanted to be comfortable sitting in a room with others. Whatever the goal is, I attempt to do everything in my power to help them reach it.

I find that when I'm able to do these three things—see, accept, and then join—the client heals.

This framework can be very helpful on many levels. As a professor, I can scaffold my students' training on it. As a counselor, when I'm picking up that something isn't right between me and the client, I can recede to its structure to find a way back. As a client myself, I can use it to evaluate whether the counselor I'm seeing is a good fit, and when there's something wrong, I can figure out if it's something that can be fixed or if I need to find a different counselor.

Wounded 2

Rader

By high school, my eating disorder was in high gear. As I've said, addiction runs in my family, and one of the most common addictions we had was to food. In fact, every member of my nuclear family (mom, dad, and two sisters) had a food addiction.

As part of our family food addiction, my mother and father were always putting all of us on the latest fad diet. It was the late 1980s, and Slim Fast was new on the market. It was all the rage. The plan for everyone in our family was a shake for breakfast, a shake for lunch, and a sensible dinner, just as the commercials said.

The second week of this diet, my biology class was having a pizza party that Friday. I reasoned that if I skipped the sensible meals during the week prior, I'd save enough calories to eat the pizza. The next week, I decided to continue the plan, allowing for an occasional binge. But the binge never came.

Within a month, I had reduced my caloric intake to one shake every other day. That's 180 calories every two days. I dropped weight like crazy, about 40 pounds in six weeks. Everyone noticed. My dating potential skyrocketed.

My parents would show me off to their friends.

One week when I weighed in at the pediatrician, the doctor, astonished at my weight loss, grabbed me by the shoulders, looked deep into my eyes, and told me, "Whatever you're doing, keep doing it.... you look great!" Not one person in my life shared any concern.

It was inevitable that I could not sustain this long term, and soon the bingeing returned. I put on about 20 pounds a year for the remaining years of high school.

The Rader Institute

My freshman year of college, I met Amber. My older sister and I both attended the same college and shared a room in a townhouse, renting out the other bedroom. Amber was one of our renters for a few months.

It didn't take long for me to realize Amber was bulimic. My reaction was extreme jealousy. I always wanted to be able to throw up, but my body was extremely resistant to letting go of food.

After a few months, Amber moved out into her own apartment, but we continued being friends. Soon I shared my own food addiction with her, and we began to binge together. She coached me on how to throw up. Amber had been doing it so long, since she was eight, that it was effortless for her. Even just leaning over was enough to trigger her vomit reflex. Not mine. I'd stick my fingers down my throat, usually pretty far back. I'd heave, usually just enough to vomit my last few bites. I was never able to expel the whole meal. I began to supplement my attempts with copious amounts of laxatives.

I soon discovered a medication called ipecac syrup that was used to induce vomiting. This was back when it was widely recommended for homes with toddlers (it's no longer widely available). Considering it a godsend, I soon was shoplifting it every week from drug stores and using it to kickstart my binges. I would combine it with a daily regimen of laxatives.

As it turns out, chronic use of ipecac syrup is extremely dangerous. It can even cause death.

Somehow my mother found out I was bingeing and purging with ipecac, and when I visited home during Thanksgiving, she took me to her therapist for an intervention. (By now, things had deteriorated in my family, and the stigma of seeing a local mental health counselor was gone.) I was told in no uncertain terms that I would be attending a residential treatment center called the Rader Institute in Florida.

I had heard of residential treatment for eating disorders before, from sources like afterschool specials, but I didn't really know what it entailed. I learned I was going to be there for four weeks over winter break from my freshman year of college. I had to contact my professors for the spring semester, as I was going to miss the first 10 days of class.

Knowing what I know now, I'm guessing it was probably recommended to my family that I take a following semester off to focus on my recovery. But that would have required them to acknowledge I was ill, which would have made the family look bad. So instead the directive was to attend treatment, get fixed quickly, and resume school without interruption. I was 17 at the time, still a minor, and didn't have much choice.

The Rader Institute was located in central Florida, in a women's hospital that also had a birthing center and breast center. Thinking back, I wanted help but didn't know how to ask for it. Most of my days were miserable, but I had no vocabulary to describe it, much less to reach out for help.

The Rader Institute used an abstinence-based, 12-step treatment approach, common of most treatment centers at the time. For eating disorders, the 12-step program is called Overeaters Anonymous, or OA. It's modeled after the original 12-step program, Alcoholics Anonymous (AA), which guides people with alcohol use disorder to accept their malady as a disease, trust in a spiritual Higher Power, and work through their "character defects" that cause them trouble in their relationships and life. In OA, the definition shifts from one with an alcohol use disorder, to one with an eating disorder. Binges are identified as the addictive behavior, and abstinence is defined as controlled, planned, healthy eating. The 12 steps of OA help people with eating disorders recognize they have an addiction to food, and then apply the spiritual program of AA to treat it.

The Rader Institute was my first introduction to such a program. All the hope I had that I could get help and get better drained out of me when staff shared the 12 Steps of Overeaters Anonymous. They were on a poster on every wall of the treatment center. My eyes read each step in order. The first step says that we have an addiction to food and that our lives had become unmanageable. Yes, this made sense to look at bulimia this way. My bingeing and purging felt out of control and my life was a mess. The second step says that we come to realize there is a power outside of ourselves that would help us. I tilted my head and squinted my eyes with apprehension and read on. Step Three is: We made a decision to turn our will over to the care of God as we understood Him. At the mention of God, my hope dropped like a lead balloon. By this time in my life, I hadn't figured out I was gay yet, but I'd known I was an atheist since I was four.

Growing up in the Bible-belt South, every family had to go to church, and I remember being four years old, sitting in the pew next to my parents and sisters, listening to the pastor, and thinking, *I just don't get it*. The idea of God just made no sense to me. But again, growing up in the Bible-belt South, I also knew never to tell anyone this. So when the treatment center told me that God was the answer, I didn't say anything, but I knew it would never work. I soon accepted the fact that I was not going to find my solution here.

Treatment consisted of daily therapy groups, psychoeducation, exercise in the form of walking every morning, and monitored meals. I finished the 28-day program and returned to my freshman year of college. The treatment did help me stop purging, but I continued to binge eat.

Over the next decade and a half, I would add 140 pounds to my frame, reaching a top weight of 325 pounds. Now I've come to understand that this fat served a very valuable purpose in my life. Most people experience an aversion to fat people, seeing them as disgusting and therefore avoiding most kinds of engagement with them. I came to depend on this stigma and weight bias. In this way, I was able to keep people at a distance. I was incapable of any kind of emotional, psychological, or physical intimacy—with friends, family, or the women I dated—for the next two decades. My fat was my protective cocoon.

Healing 3

BYOLAA!

Sometime in my 20s, I began to personify my eating disorder. It had become something I hated and loathed. My body was becoming large, and my belly started to hang down in a thick curtain of fat. I wanted to find a name for my stomach that really spoke to the ugliness and hatred I felt for it.

The ugliest name I could think of was Beulah. It just sounds horrible. So, Beulah became the monster that lived in me. She'd call out and demand attention, and I was a slave to her. When the craving for a binge came, I imagined the call coming from the monster within me, and I had to appease Beulah. I'd be in class, and Beulah would call out, "Feed me." I'd be sitting in a session with a client, and Beulah would cry, "I'm hungry." Beulah convinced me to isolate and ignore all my needs in the name of a binge. She was with me every morning, all day, and all night. She could demand my attention at any time. There was nothing in my life she couldn't disrupt. We had a very abusive relationship.

In my mid-30s, after about five years of therapy, my therapist helped me understand that as a child, what I was always seeking from my parents was love, approval, and acceptance, and despite their best efforts I had never truly felt any of these things. She told me, "You will need to learn to bring your own love, approval, and acceptance to yourself as an adult."

That really rang with me. "Bring Your Own Love, Approval, and Acceptance" became a battle cry for me. Contemplating this sentiment one day, I thought it might be helpful to develop an acronym I could use to remind me that this was my job. "Bring Your Own Love, Approval, and Acceptance." I wrote out the first letters from each of the words: B-Y-O-L-A-A. *What would that sound like,* I wondered? I started to sound out the letters. *Bee-Yuu-Ooo-Laa-Aaa-Aaa. Bee-you-laa.* Putting the sounds together, I said them out loud. "Bee-you-laa. Be-yu-lah. Beulah." It dawned on me the acronym sounds exactly like the horrible name I had picked out for my stomach. I sat for a few minutes and marveled at the coincidence.

Everything inside me shifted. I suddenly realized that Beulah was not this monster demanding subservience, worthy of hatred and disdain. Beulah was the little kid in me who just wanted to be acknowledged and celebrated for who she was. When she demanded a binge, it was only because she didn't have the skills to ask for what she really needed. She was the part of me that desperately wanted to be loved. To be held, to be seen, to be comforted. That's who Beulah really was. I learned that day that when Beulah called out for my attention, she wasn't asking for food; she was asking for love, approval, and acceptance.

It took me some time to learn to answer the call differently, but since that day I've learned to use the new rallying cry: "BYOLAA!"

Healing 4

Enough

Enough is an interesting word for addicts like me. I've learned we travel through three phases of *enough* in our journey from addiction to healing.

1. The first phase is our quest for *enough drugs*.
2. The second phase is deciding we've experienced *enough consequences* and are ready to try something different.
3. And the third phase appears when we get sober and learn that *we are enough*, and always have been.

The first phase: *enough drugs*. When we're using, we're always looking for more, more, more. There is never enough of our drug of choice. Now to be sure, it's always our goal to have enough, but we never get there. Enough is a distant, far-off land. We'll get part of the way there but miss the target, and this fuels our desire to try over and over again.

There's actually a little bit of biology happening here. Usually, a person's first high is their most intense. Their brain's chemistry was unprepared for the flood of this drug, so their system produces a maximum response, usually a hugely pleasurable dopamine dump. People experience this as the most intense high of their life. And then they spend the rest of their using careers trying to replicate it.

But because our brains have neuroplasticity, they adapt to the substance. They learn to quickly release countermeasures to tamp down the effects of the drug. This means the user can never experience that first high again. It's a biological impossibility.

But we try. Boy do we try.

The second phase: *enough consequences*. The journey to recovery must cross a threshold where the individual decides they've had enough of the using life. Enough relationship problems. Enough work or school penalties. Enough legal issues. Enough mental health illness. Enough watching hurting people expressing their concerns to us, again and again, to the point where they leave us.

To an outsider, watching an addict travel from first use to *enough consequences* is witnessing a journey through insanity. Certainly, no sane person would do what we do—building up wreckage and consequences, and then doubling down for more. Every person with a substance use disorder has their journey through this. The fundamental definition of addiction is continuing to use some substance or behavior despite increasingly negative consequences. This is, indeed, the core of addiction.

Many people never finish this part of the journey. They die trying. But some reach a point where they've had enough.

Much of a counselor's job is working with the client to transition them from the dimension of *never enough* to the dimension of *I've had enough*. This is the essence of a counseling technique called *motivational interviewing*, which is based on a theory called *stages of change*. Dr. David Mee-Lee, a psychiatrist and widely considered a guru of addiction counseling, outlines the following: a lot of people end up in treatment, and we start giving them recovery treatment work. Treatment plans on how to stay sober. Relapse prevention work. But the client is not there yet. Dr. Mee-Lee asserts what this person needs is not a *"recovery"* program, but a *"discovery"* program. Here, they are helped to become aware and explore their past behaviors and their consequences to get them to the point of having had enough. Only once they have reached a point of enough consequences can they entertain this new path of recovery. *That's* when we introduce the recovery treatment work.

And again, watching someone go through this journey and not quite getting there, going back out again and again, ending up in treatment after treatment, or jail after jail, or hospital after hospital, is excruciating. That is, if you don't understand the journey of an addict.

A lot of the work I do is helping student counselors understand that this is *part* of the journey to healing, and we are here not to stop it, but to guide clients through it. Counselors who spin out—becoming exasperated watching patient after patient leave treatment and then return to use, without understanding this fundamental idea—burn out pretty quickly. I also help families of loved ones learn how to survive this torturous period. Family members who don't understand how to take care of themselves while their loved one is on this part of their journey develop their own mental health and relationship issues. Learning appropriate inner and outer boundaries, along with acceptance and respect for this process, is key to longevity in this profession, and personal sanity.

For some people, this part of the journey is relatively short. A couple of years of consequences is all they need. But some people need more. Sometimes decades more. When they are in treatment, I work with clients to help them understand they have a choice: do they need to go out and get more consequences, or are they ready to discover they hold the power to make the consequences stop? The choice is entirely theirs, and I don't judge either one. Because until a person thoroughly and deeply believes the consequences aren't going to stop, and that there's no such thing as using without consequences, they *need* to go back out and "do more research." My goal in this case is to prepare the client to minimize their potential harm in going back out. But I don't try to manipulate them, or try to convince them to stay, pretty please. And I certainly don't judge, shame, or look down at them for leaving. I don't even feel bad or get scared. I understand they are still on their *enough* journey. I do always have hope, though. I hope that the rest of their journey is short and I hope that they make it back to treatment somewhere.

The third phase: *I am enough.* The moment an addict concludes that they've had enough, the journey of recovery begins. And ultimately, the end goal of this journey is to learn that they are enough. Who they are is enough. And that they've always been enough.

Here, they learn there's no need to seek outside sources to feel like enough. The journey to enough does not go through the accumulation of booze, or drugs, or food, or possessions, or whatever else someone has been ingesting, or buying, or doing. Happiness, contentment, and peace all come from within, and the source is already present in every person. There's no need to seek anything outward. Everything they need is within. We just need to connect them to it.

The other way this lack of being enough shows up for addicts is in their experience of a lifelong belief that they're somehow deficient or inferior. That they must earn love and approval from others to prove that they're good enough. They may think, *If I can just get someone to love me, or to tell me I'm doing a good job, or give me some award, or elect me to some position, this will show me that I'm enough.* And many addicts achieve these things. But it never works. They never feel like enough.

In recovery, they finally learn that *who they are* is enough. Just by being born—and being authentically who they are—they are enough. There's nothing they need to do, to earn, to prove, in order to be considered enough. We counselors lightly remind our clients that we are *human beings*, not *human doings*. Just by virtue of being human, we have worth.

This is a long circuitous healing journey, from can't get enough, to enough consequences, to I am enough. Most of America is programmed to find themselves on some part of this journey, with our core values of achievement and consumerism. We are taught from birth that we must *earn* our place in this world, and we do so by seeking accolades, prizes, and wealth. This is one of the reasons that America is often seen as one of the most successful countries in the world. It's also, however, one of the reasons why America is one of the most addicted countries in the world. We consume more illicit drugs than any other country. Many writers have made this connection, none quite as eloquently as Anna Lembke, MD, in her book *Dopamine Nation*.

When people in recovery rooms are talking about their addiction, most aren't referring to their substance use at all. They're referring to this pathway. Most participants in a 12-step meeting will introduce themselves by name, and then include their identifier: "and I'm an alcoholic," "and I'm an addict," "and I'm a compulsive overeater," "and I'm in recovery," etc. One time I was at a meeting and a person introduced themselves as "and I'm addicted to *MORE.*" Every single head in the room nodded knowingly. We all understood.

Wounded 3

Pre-Prac

I wasn't supposed to get into grad school.

After I was introduced to 12-step recovery at age 17, I ran like hell. My early 20s were spent just getting by. I graduated college with a Classics degree and taught high school in North Carolina for two years before moving to Chicago with my sister on a whim. Then I bounced around with temp jobs for a year, finally settling into an administrative job at a public relations firm and making what felt like good money after the paltry salary of a North Carolina teacher. My sister soon decided she wanted to go into the military, and within two years, she had enlisted in the Coast Guard and was off to Cape May, New Jersey, for basic training. I was left alone in Chicago. I had no friends, and my life consisted of work, takeout, binges, and TV shows.

One weekend, I flew to New Hampshire to visit my mother. My sister met us there. We went out to lunch, and my mother and sister sat across from me. It was clear they had been conspiring.

"We think you want to go to graduate school. We suspect you want to study psychology. We're here to help make it happen," they announced.

I hadn't been thinking about it at all, but really, I had nothing else going on, so that's what I did. I spent a lot of my 20s doing what other people wanted me to do. I wasn't able to get in touch with anything inside of me, but instead just internalized other people's desires and made them my own. So I returned to Chicago and began exploring graduate programs in psychology.

The problem was I had never taken a psychology class in my life. I had consciously stayed away from them in undergraduate for fear that I would find out exactly how messed up I was. I had ended up getting a bachelor's degree in Latin, so all my coursework was ancient history and classical languages. And I didn't graduate with a good GPA. All of this didn't bode well for my chances of getting into a psychology graduate program.

But at all my temp jobs during my first year in Chicago, on Monday mornings, I was always the one who people lined up to share about their weekends. They sought me out to reflect on what was going on in their lives, and to help them figure out how to solve their problems. People seemed to like my guidance and advice. Everywhere I went, people told me, "You should be a psychologist." Although I could recognize a natural talent, I still had quite the learning curve to overcome.

I spent about six months investigating graduate programs. I learned there were different specializations in psychology. There was clinical psychology, which focuses on the assessment, diagnosis, and treatment of mental health disorders. There was counseling psychology, which facilitates personal and interpersonal functioning throughout the lifespan. Forensic psychology involves working with individuals in the law and legal system. Industrial-organizational psychology studies human behavior in the workplace.

Educational psychology studies how humans learn. And there are many, many other specializations. It was overwhelming to sort out.

I also learned almost all graduate programs wanted their students to come in with a developed research interest. It could be a population the student desired to work with, or a research track they wanted to follow.

I developed the vaguest idea of what I wanted to study. Having worked two years as a high school teacher, I was interested in learning how teachers balanced all the stresses of teaching with low pay and demanding parents. In this way, clinical and counseling programs made the most sense for my pursuit. I didn't have the academic vocabulary to describe my interests, but I was determined to try to get into a program anyway.

I visited various open houses at schools all over the Midwest. Most schools were dismissive of me. It was clear I did not fit their profile of a prospective student. I also contacted individual professors and asked for meetings. One such professor was at the University of Illinois at Champaign-Urbana. His research focused on studying happiness. I felt this was loosely connected to what I was interested in. After badgering him for a meeting, he begrudgingly invited me to come to his office hour. Excited to finally have a lead, I took the day off work, rented a car, and drove the two and a half hours south to Champaign, Illinois.

We only talked for about 15 minutes. I described, in my fumbling vocabulary, my interest in studying teachers' stress. He cut me off and told me I should go down to the School of Education. I thought he misunderstood my interests, thinking I wanted to be a school counselor.

"No," I said. "I don't want to be a school counselor; I want to study the lives of teachers." He kept insisting that is where I should be.

I walked out of the Psychology building feeling defeated and disappointed. What a wasted use of paid time off.

Out of curiosity, I looked at the campus map. The Education building was a half mile south. The weather was perfect, 70 degrees and sunny, so I decided, *Why not at least walk down there?* I had the car until 10 p.m., and I had made quite an effort to get there. *What's another 30 minutes?*

Dr. Brene Brown, a noted researcher and thought leader in my field, and others talk about "sliding door" moments in life, when seemingly simple little choices affect a person in big ways. This was mine. My whole life changed, because it was a nice day outside. Had it been raining, or cold, or some other weather, I would have hopped in the rental car and returned home. And my life today would be completely different.

It's funny how the littlest things can change the course of a life.

I found the department of educational psychology on the second floor and met its administrative assistant. We struck up a delightful conversation. In a bizarre coincidence, it turns out we were from the same small podunk town in North Carolina. We bonded instantly. I described to her the vague and unformed ideas I had about what I wanted to study.

She excitingly said, "Oh, that's counseling psychology. That's one of the four divisions of educational psychology. You should definitely apply to that." It turns out that counseling psychology departments, while rarely studying educational psychology issues, are often housed in colleges of education.

And so I did apply, while also sending Hail Mary applications to 13 other schools. Most schools outright rejected my application for lack of appropriate undergraduate preparation. But my GRE scores were stellar, so this warranted further action from some schools.

To illustrate how little I knew about the field, when asked to submit a review of a professional article for one application, I selected an article about a psychologist named Albert Ellis in a magazine called *Counseling Today*. I had no idea that there were these things called academic journals where research was published. This is the equivalent of submitting a review of a *People* magazine article when asked to comment on the latest in literature. I can only laugh now at the reactions the admissions committee must have had to my essay.

But for some reason, I managed to get an interview with the counseling psychology doctoral program at the University of Illinois, the one I had visited on a whim. I went that January.

It was a full-day interview, filled with multiple meetings with current faculty and students. I really had no idea what I was doing, and I certainly didn't have the language to carry on an erudite conversation with academics. But I knew I generally interviewed well, and one professor there had research interests I could sort of align with. I fumbled along as best I could.

I ended up on the waitlist for admission. Then one of their accepted students decided to go to the University of Maryland, and poof, I was in. I wanted to send that student a bouquet of flowers!

(Years later, at the end of my program, I was attending a class with the head of the department. Somehow the conversation among us turned to how we each had come to this university. The department head cocked his head to one side and looked at me.

"Did I ever tell you how you got in?" he asked.

"No," I answered, but I was very interested—now knowing how unlikely it was that a student without the right undergraduate preparation would be admitted to a top tier university. He said that year, every time the faculty requested the files of the applicants, the administrative assistant I had struck up a conversation with always put my file on top and advocated for me. "She's a diamond in the rough, that one," she'd tell them. Again, you never know how a chance encounter can change the course of your life. Eventually, she wore them down and they agreed to put me on the waitlist.)

Once admitted, I knew I had a lot of catching up to do. I decided to leave my job in Chicago to move down to Champaign early and audit a couple of undergraduate summer psychology classes. Having spent five years out in the real world, where work was nine to five and your boss structured your time, I knew I had to reacclimate to the rhythms and demands of being a student. Plus, I had to fill in my missing undergraduate psychology background. I took Psych 100: Introduction to Psychology, and an introduction to statistics. I read everything assigned in the classes, was an active and inquisitive participant in all discussions, and completed all the homework and tests. It was a serious crash course in the foundations of psychology, and I was determined to do my best.

I succeeded in the crash course, and I began the first semester in my program. That fall was a blur. I focused hard on my studies, and by the end of the semester, I was starting to pull my weight with the other students in my cohort. My writing had dramatically improved and was now starting to sound academic.

That spring, I began a class called "pre-practicum." Its purpose was to teach basic counseling skills to prepare students for their first clinical placement the following fall. The class used volunteer clients, and we'd each meet with that client for five counseling sessions. Each session was videotaped and reviewed by student supervisors. When we met with our supervisor each week to watch the tapes together, they would stop and hit pause at times to point out things they noticed. "Why did you ask this question right then?" or "Look at how the body language of the client shifts here" were the kinds of things they would say. The program aimed to begin developing what are called *counseling microskills*—like active listening, reflecting, and summarizing—that form the foundation of all therapy.

This class scared the crap out of me. From the moment I signed up for it the previous semester, I felt an eerie dread. I just knew I had to prove myself as worthy. After all, I had gotten into this program by the skin of my teeth. I might be able to bring up my academic skills to a graduate level, but this was a whole different beast. This wasn't about academic smarts, which I knew I had. This involved actually counseling someone. Showing that I could connect and help.

My imposter syndrome reared its head and began overwhelming me. I knew, just knew, that my supervisor was going to view my tapes and come to the conclusion that I shouldn't continue pursuing my degree. This was going to escalate up to the dean, and I'd be asked to leave the program. My dream of a doctorate would be over. No other school would have me, I was sure.

So I set about on a mission. I was going to *fix* this client. If I could make this person's life better, they'd have to let me stay. My client was a volunteer from an introductory psychology class, a young man whose presenting concern was adjusting to a being a student at a large college. In his first session, I made all the mistakes beginning counselors make: I talked more than the client, I jumped way too soon to solutions, and I didn't show many microskills. And my supervisor gave me this feedback, as was appropriate.

However, I was crushed and interpreted the feedback as suggesting I was a horrible counselor. This started the most intense shame spiral of my life.

The next two sessions weren't much better. My client no-showed for the last two sessions. I couldn't blame him. My imposter syndrome and shame spiral had kept us from connecting.

The whole experience, to me, was just traumatizing. But I managed to pass the class.

In hindsight, now that I'm a professor, I see that my difficulty in learning counseling skills isn't all that uncommon for students; in fact, it's pretty standard. But I didn't know that and continued to carry my deep shame and feelings of worthlessness into the summer.

At the end of the course, I was assigned to the university counseling center for my first real placement. Come fall, I'd have real clients. I churned in fear all summer. *There's no way I can subject real clients with real issues to my horrible counseling*, I told myself.

From the first day of the program, as a matter of course, the head of the department offered to supply students with names of local therapists. It's very common for psychology graduate students to go through their own course of therapy during their training years. As a dutiful student, I took him up on his offer and got three names my first semester. But I never called them. I was too scared at what they might uncover. Instead, I spent the endless summer nights tossing and turning, trying to figure out what to do. I couldn't report to this placement, but I couldn't not report, either.

At two a.m. one night, about two weeks before I was due to report, I composed an email to my academic advisor saying that I needed to drop out of the program. It was the only solution I could come up with.

My advisor, wisely, called me in for a meeting and asked me what was up. I confessed my terror at starting to see real clients. I told her I was no good at this. She patiently listened to me. And then she made a proposal. What if I sat out on clinicals this year and started my own personal therapy, working on myself so I could eventually feel comfortable starting practicum? This would delay my practicum by a year, but I could switch out the practicum class for an academic one. She said this so calmly and straightforwardly.

I was flabbergasted. I had just told this esteemed academic I was no good, but she seemed to see something in me. What was it? I couldn't find it myself.

I picked up that list of therapists again and worked through it. The first one never called me back. The second one had no openings. The third one was Peggy.

The day I made that phone call to Peggy is the day I started my path to recovery. I still had a long way to go before I felt healed, but that was the day the process started.

I worked with Peggy for the next six years. Pretty early on, she started talking to me about the impact of growing up in a dysfunctional family. She told me I wasn't crazy for thinking all the thoughts I did. She recommended I read Dr. Claudia Black's *Changing Courses*. Here, on page after page, I read my story. And this is where I learned the three rules of an alcoholic family, which as I've mentioned, applied to my family: Don't Talk, Don't Trust, Don't Feel. Then Peggy began gently suggesting I attend a 12-step meeting called Overeaters Anonymous. *The one with all the God stuff?*

"Thanks, but it's not for me," I responded.

Peggy continued working on me. Every time I brought up a new issue, she softly suggested that 12-step recovery might be a good place to work on it. And every time, I resisted. I came up with excuse after excuse about why this program wasn't for me.

"Check out a few meetings," she encouraged. "What's the harm?"

Still, I persisted. The memories of the OA meetings I'd gone to in treatment were strong.

But Peggy was patient. Finally, after a year and I half, she wore me down. I had developed enough trust in her that I was willing to take a chance. I looked up a local meeting on Thursday nights and made a plan to attend. And I went.

Boy, was Peggy right.

That first OA meeting I went to was called a *Big Book* study meeting. The *Big Book* is the foundational text for most 12-step recovery programs. It was written by the founders of Alcoholics Anonymous in the 1930s and 1940s, and had gone through several revisions by the time I joined. It outlined the basics of 12-step recovery, and included many different stories of members' paths through addiction and into recovery. The agenda for each meeting was to read a chapter of the Big Book and then discuss how it applied to our food addictions.

I heard other people talk about food the way I thought about food. The incessant obsessions about what they were going to binge on. The deep disgust they felt about themselves afterward. The lengths they went through to hide their eating. The ways they neglected other people to keep their food addictions going. During announcements, one member shared about a retreat that weekend an hour away. I had no plans that weekend, so I went. (I didn't know that most people new to OA don't go to retreats right away. I went on my third day in the program.)

During one of the breakout sessions, people were sharing on the topic of selfishness. One woman shared a recent experience. She had been a bridesmaid for her sister's wedding. Her dress was sleeveless. She shared how self-absorbed she was because the whole day, all she could think about was how her arms looked in the dress. She was so obsessed with this thought that she wasn't present for her sister's big day. She spoke about being there, but not really being there. There was such sadness in her voice.

I'd never heard anyone talk like this. I'd never thought that my constant focus on my appearance was a selfish act. Yet I constantly compared my physical appearance to everyone else in the room. I was always aware if I was the biggest person, which I usually was.

Describing this behavior as *self-centeredness*—that blew my mind. And it made all the sense in the world. *What else do these people think?* I wondered. This was not all the God talk I'd heard before. This actually made sense.

The meeting changed my life. The date was January 22, 2004. In the 20 years since, I've never gone more than three weeks without a 12-step meeting. I've been a member of five different groups in three different states: Overeaters Anonymous, CoDependents Anonymous, Al-Anon, Alcoholics Anonymous, and Narcotics Anonymous. I wasn't able to get sober for another 11 years, but I kept coming back. I knew there was something there. And I wanted to hear more.

Healing 5

Mom.

Many years ago, I gathered with my mother, sisters, and brother-in-law at my older sister's house. At this point, we were all adults living in different states, so it was special when we could get together. Playing cards or board games was common during these times together.

Some time prior to this, my father, in a vain attempt to create a closer family, had given my sister a board game that was designed for various generations in a family to bond. Players would move pieces on the game board, with the goal of progressing to the center. Along the way, different spots required players to share a story about their life, such as where they went to high school or what their first car was. They could also share stories about pivotal moments, like when they felt the happiest. The goal was to share family memories and make it to the center of the board. When each player crossed the finish line, the reward was that every member would share their favorite memory of that player. It was totally hokey, but we decided to try and play it out of irony. Our family was obviously not the intended audience for this game.

We took our turns along the winding path. Each of us landed on various spaces and shared little memories. As luck would have it, I crossed the finish line first. It was time for my reward, for each family member to share their favorite memory of me.

My little sister, sitting to my right, shared a memory of something funny that had happened when we attended summer camp one year. Next it was my mother's turn.

"J," she said, pausing to take in a deep breath, then exhaling, "You were my most difficult child . . ."

"Mom," my little sister howled, "the goal is to share your *happiest* memory!"

The point was made. My mother and I didn't have many happy memories.

I'd always had a complicated relationship with my mother. I just never found her to be on my side. When I was a child, I rarely received warmth and acceptance from her. Most of the time I spent in her presence was stressful. I've thought a lot about the origins of this discord. I think it goes back to my very beginning.

My mother was born right at the beginning of the baby boom generation. She reached her teenage years in the late 1950s and early 1960s. The women's liberation movement had not yet begun. As a result, society gave my mother very strict and strong messages on what a good woman was: "be nice, modest, thin, and use all available resources for appearance," as Brene Brown says. My mom was taught to marry young, produce children, and prioritize taking care of her children and husband as her life's work.

My mother was stick thin when she was a girl, a fact she often shared with us as we were growing up. She seemed to make this comment to contrast her body with mine and my sisters', which were decidedly not thin. She had internalized the societal messages of the ideal female body, and was obsessed with her weight and appearance. She grew up as a Navy brat, moving and acclimating to a new community and culture every two years—including Hawaii, California, Texas, and Oregon. That's a lot of different cultures to adjust to. Being very attractive facilitated easier entrance to a new social group each time.

She was smart and ended up graduating high school early at age 16. Her father had retired from active duty in the Navy by then, and he relocated his family back to his childhood home of Pamlico County, North Carolina. Soon after, she met my father. After what was described as a three-month whirlwind courtship, he proposed and she accepted.

There was just one problem: my mother's family despised my father's family and forbade the union. Because she was under 18 and needed parental consent to marry, this made a marriage impossible. But my parents persisted, and two years later, just three days after my mother's 18th birthday, they got married. Neither of her parents attended.

Choosing my father created a deep rift between my mother and her family. My mother dealt with it by doubling down on my father, dedicating every minute of her life to making him successful. She helped put him through the remainder of his undergraduate degree, and then through law school at the University of North Carolina. When they moved back to the North Carolina coast, he began his law career and established himself as a capable lawyer—first as a public defender, and then as a defense attorney. He formed an independent firm with a couple of other lawyers.

It was then time to have children. During her pregnancy with my older sister, my mother hypercontrolled her diet. She weighed and measured everything she ate and limited her diet. She gained very little weight and maintained a petite, attractive figure. As a result, when my mom was 25, my sister was born at a barely normal weight. My mother used to amusingly talk about how her limbs were skinny little sticks.

About a year later, my mother became pregnant with me. For some reason, she treated my pregnancy very differently. She ate anything and everything she wanted. She would describe times when she would sit down with an entire chocolate, frosted cake and a fork and devour it all in one sitting.

She was given a customer-favorite booth at a nearby diner on the beach. She frequently ate breakfast there—tons of eggs, hash browns, and pancakes. As a result, she put on more than 80 pounds during this pregnancy. And I was born 33 percent larger than my sister, at eight pounds even, with rolls of fat along my arms and legs. My mother used to shamingly tease me with descriptions of how she had to pull apart the rolls of fat to bathe between them.

I realized a few years ago that this pregnancy was the first time in her life that my mother ever felt "overweight." I sensed how difficult this must have been for her. All my life, my mother had obsessed about her weight, and even a few extra pounds was a source of distress and deep shame. And my father loved showing off his beautiful wife.

What must she have thought about me? I wondered. I was the reason she was "fat." She had spent her entire life being attractive; with the extra weight from my pregnancy, which she was never able to entirely get rid of, she was no longer svelte, petite, or eye-catching. I knew from a young age that, for my mother, being overweight was a source of deep shame and feelings of worthlessness. And this all happened because she was pregnant with me.

Now, I don't think this was a conscious thought at all, but I do believe my mother somehow attached feeling bad about herself to my existence. On a subconscious level, I was to blame for her lost attractiveness. I believe this colored our relationship for my whole life, and prevented us from forming a bond. If under every interaction with me lay subconscious feelings of worthlessness, how could a mother possibly bond with her child?

I want to stop here and make a point that I do not blame my mother for any of this. It was not her fault that she attached this connection to me. She was bombarded with messages every day of her existence that equated her appearance to her worth. She had had many life experiences that reinforced this message. I'm simply acknowledging that this is what I think happened.

In the end, my parents had three children, all girls. My mother passed on her attachment to weight to all of us. Lessons on *slimness* came early and often.

In middle childhood, we would ride our bikes all over town. We were greeted at the end of each trip by my mother at the front door, who would inspect us to make sure we weren't bringing in any candy. Quickly we found a workaround; each of us would purchase a bag of candy from the gas station in town, and stealthily place it outside on our windowsills. Then we would come in through the front door, pass my mother's inspection, and each go to our rooms, alone, to binge on the candy. Disordered eating happened very early in my family.

I matured early, getting my period at age nine. I started to develop breasts. One day, my mother told us that every woman should be able to jump up and down in front of a mirror, and the only thing that should jiggle should be our breasts. I internalized this test deeply, using it over the decades as proof that I was not attractive. Never once did I pass this test. I usually jiggled everywhere.

My relationship with my mother remained distant at best throughout my adolescence and young adulthood. During many periods, it was downright hostile.

I spent most of my childhood and adolescence looking for any and every opportunity to be away from my family. By age 10, I took every offer to babysit for local families. I started formally working outside the home when I was 12. And I got into a prestigious residential magnet school at 15. Students lived there during the school year; it was located three hours away, a distance which suited me just fine. While I attended this school, my parents downsized and bought a house with fewer bedrooms. My bedroom was the one that was eliminated. With literally no place for me at home after that, I essentially left home when I was 15.

My independence continued. I went straight to college from high school, getting special permission to enter summer school two weeks after high school graduation. After two years, I was selected for a student exchange program with the University of Edinburgh, and lived abroad my junior year in Scotland. I came back, completed my remaining classes, and graduated. I found a teaching job in a rural high school close to back home, and moved there.

My relationship with my mother began to change when I was 22.

After 32 years of marriage, one day my father came home and told my mother, "I don't love you. I never have." He stated they were getting a divorce. My mother was devastated. Her whole world was crumbling. She'd spent her entire life building up his career and raising their children. She'd yielded to his every desire and plan, and frankly was a primary reason for his success. In the process, she was living her life through him.

Upon announcing his desire for a divorce, my father expected my mother to slink away silently, find a little apartment in a nearby town, and live a quiet existence. My mother had other ideas.

For the next five years, she fought for a fair settlement. My father was socially connected to almost every judge in their half of the state, so she was fighting against a whole legal system. Still, she refused to leave their house—a beautiful cottage-style by a little pond on a 100-acre property we called "the farm."

In the process, my father moved to a visitor's shack on the property about 100 yards away from the house. They lived like this for three years. My sisters and I were very intentional in making sure we spent time with both parents, and deftly avoided any conversations about the other parent. Still, going home for a visit was like preparing to enter a to-the-death battle zone.

But one thing had definitely changed. During these three years, I saw my mother come alive. She took no bullshit. She fought tooth and nail for everything she was entitled to. She went back to school and finished her undergraduate degree (she had left college earlier, when Dad graduated law school, because he was ready to go). She even continued on to graduate school and began a master's program in finance, determined to learn how to be financially independent.

During this time, watching her, I began to build respect. I lived 45 minutes away, so I frequently visited during the weekends to see how she was doing. I also plainly saw how this new superwoman approach definitely was taking a toll on her. She was exhausted at times from having to fight her legal battle, and from maintaining her composure every time she drove past my dad's shack.

After a while, Dad had the woman he was involved with during his last affair move in with him.

At times, my mom would break down in tears with me. Behind the tears was a determined gaze in her eyes. She definitely presented a warrior shield—only giving me peeks at the fragility underneath.

But at one event, I got to fully see all of her. One weekend, I had convinced her to leave the property. She rarely left; she was just too tired and depressed to do so. But this weekend, she had agreed to come visit my apartment on the beach for one night. As I drove to pick her up, I felt happy she would finally get a break from her battle.

She had gotten a dog, a standard schnauzer named Archie that she had bonded deeply to by this time. He was her primary support, and was unwaveringly loyal and attached to her.

"I haven't seen Archie in a while," she announced as she finished her packing. This wasn't unusual. The property was large, and all the pets often roamed free.

Venturing outside, I began to call his name. I circled the house, and strolled out onto the dock. And then I saw him. Just into the deep water of the pond, his little body was sideways and floating—curved, definitely dead. I could feel the color drain from my face. I knew I needed to go in and tell my mother that Archie—her 24/7 companion and support—was dead.

I returned her bedroom. I actually don't remember telling her, but I vividly remember what happened next. My mother let out a small gasp as the reality settled onto her. Then a look came over her. I had never seen it before. It was both deeply wounded and deeply determined.

My mother exited the house with purpose—heading out onto the dock, and then stepping down to the pond. She was wearing a nice outfit, slacks and a summer blouse, but that didn't change her next steps. She descended into the pond and waded out to where the dog was, about waist high. Then she scooped him up—all 40 pounds of him, his body stiff with early rigor mortis. After turning around, she began a determined walk back to the shore.

The dog was holding massive amounts of water in his fur; as my mother ascended from the pond, waves of water cascaded down. I didn't know what to do; I was frozen, assuming the role of witness. I somehow knew not to intervene.

My mother exited the pond and walked up the small beach to the garage at the top of the shore. She walked around to a little open area in the back. Then she put Archie down on the ground, tears streaming down her face. She went into the garage to get a shovel and came back out. She was going to bury this dog. It was something she *had* to do.

She dug a deep hole. Again, I somehow knew my role was as a witness, and I should not intervene. She cried out each time she struck the ground, shoveling heaps of dirt out methodically. At this point, her nice outfit was ruined, but I knew the outfit didn't matter; my mother was in another world. For 20 minutes, she dug, creating a three-by-two-foot foot hole, four feet deep. As the hole formed, my mother stepped in it to dig deeper. She looked a mess—covered in sweat and soaked in pond water, her hair going in every direction. Tears continued to streak down her face.

Finally, she got out of the hole and picked up Archie. She laid him down gently at the bottom of the hole, squatting there for a minute to gently stroke his fur. Then she stood and started covering him with dirt.

At the third or fourth shovelful, my mother let out a wail I will never forget. It was loud, and long. It came from deep, deep within her. It communicated all the hurt she was feeling, from everything she was going through. And I could feel all the hurt she was releasing. I was seeing my mother at her most raw, real existence.

At the time I was overwhelmed, only knowing I had never seen my mother this way before. Later, I would come to remember it as a beautiful experience. I had seen my mother at her most real. The moment remains the most intimate of our lives together.

She finished covering Archie with dirt and dropped the shovel and walked away. She said she no longer wanted to leave the property. I tried for a few minutes to get her to come with me; I was concerned for her mental health if she stayed. I really wanted to get her into a different setting. But she was determined; she wanted to stay. After 45 minutes, I respected her wishes and quietly left. I understood she needed to be there to grieve.

My relationship with my mother changed that day. As a child and adolescent, I had always seen my mother as an empty shell, someone who spent her existence trying to create the perfect—yet fake—family. She seemed more concerned with appearances than with reality. But that day, I saw my mother's core. And it was beautiful. It was powerful, determined, resolute. It did not care one bit about appearances. I was full of awe.

It took me some time to digest all that I saw that day. Through all my life struggles, I've since come to understand that I have a similar core, and that I got that from her, not my dad. Somehow, I inherited her strength and power and determination. In this, I now feel deeply connected and attached to her in a way I never had as a child.

Christmas came that year, and my sisters and I gathered with my mother to exchange presents. I presented her with a poem I had cross-stitched that had meant a lot to me. It's an abridged version of a poem by Argentinian writer and poet Jorge Luis Borges, later revised by Veronica Shoffstall:

After a while you learn the subtle difference

    between holding a hand and changing a soul

And you learn that kisses aren't contracts

    and presents aren't promises

With the grace of a woman, not the grief of a child

You learn to build your roads today

> *for tomorrow's ground is too uncertain*

Because plans and futures have a way of falling down in mid-flight

So you plant your own garden,

> *and decorate your own soul,*

instead of waiting for someone to bring you flowers

And you learn that you can endure,

> *that you really are strong,*

> *and you really do have worth,*

And you learn . . . And you learn . . . And you learn . . .

I cross-stitched a simple border with a heart motif and put it in a cheap picture frame. My mother, when she opened my gift, sat in silence as she read. Her eyes welled with tears. She quietly walked out of the room for several minutes, and when she returned, she gave me a hug. I understood that she was uncomfortable fully sharing her feelings; her discomfort with intimacy was the reason she retreated from the room for a bit. But we further deepened our connection that day, because she understood I saw the woman she was becoming.

Thirteen years later, when I ended an important romantic relationship and was surrounded by grief and shame, I received a box in the mail. It was the cross-stitched poem with a note from my mother. She explained how once upon a time, someone had given this to her in a moment when she really needed it, and that she was returning it to me in the same way. We never spoke of it, but it meant a lot to me.

My mother was able to continue her legal fight and finally got a fair settlement. She ended up moving to Atlanta to earn a second master's degree and worked for almost two decades as a financial planner. She remarried, but divorced after eight years because she was tired of taking care of a man with nothing in return.

My mom still has her issues with food, but I've been able to separate myself from that. She's retired now, living at my sister's organic dairy farm in a little one-person cottage she had built. She spends her days keeping busy: golf and crochet circles and walks. She has no desire to remarry; she says her generation of men all want to be taken care of, and she is not remotely interested in that. She does what she wants to do. I now look to her as a model of how to live in this regard.

We really have been on quite a journey, me and her.

Healing happens in a million different ways. Sometimes there is one pivotal event; sometimes it's a series of things over years. Sometimes there's a lot of talking. My relationship with my mother healed without either of us saying hardly a word.

Wounded 4

Jails, Institutions, and Death

The first time I ever had Vicodin was when I was 16, after wisdom teeth removal. I had the quintessential addict response: a feeling that all was finally right with the world, and that I was at last comfortable in it.

I was an opportunistic user for the next decade, getting prescriptions during medical appointments whenever I could, or secretly stealing a few from a medicine cabinet in a relative's or friend's house. My more salient addiction during this time was to food.

As I've outlined earlier, when I was 27, I entered a doctoral program in psychology. At 28, I started therapy. At 30, I went to my first OA meeting. The recommended year off of clinicals to start my own therapy was successful, and I resumed my clinical training at the University's counseling center. By my fourth year of school, I had developed an interest in working at the university's Alcohol and Other Drug Office.

I was mainly motivated to work with the counselor who headed the program, Amy. I was drawn to her incredible skill, along with her story of recovery from addiction. Amy would go on to serve as a mentor to me for the next five years and taught me the basics of addiction counseling.

I worked as a graduate assistant in the Alcohol and Other Drug Office for the next four years as I completed my academic training, conducting assessments for students who'd gotten into some kind of trouble for their substance use. I also led a psychoeducation workshop for students with identified problems. Very few of these students saw the assessment or workshop as anything other than punishment to be endured to maintain their status at the university.

I could feel my clinical self coming alive in this role of working with these students. I found that I had a talent for talking with people who didn't want to be in therapy, as I learned their stories and rolled with their reluctance to engage.

One day I had a client show for an assessment after receiving a marijuana ticket. He announced he was the president of the local chapter of NORML, a marijuana legalization group, and he had only consented to the assessment so he could gather data to take back to his organization to help their cause. He brought a notebook, and ostentatiously opened it and began writing notes.

I thanked him for his honesty, and said I hoped I would provide some good data. It never occurred to me to try to get him to stop taking notes. However, as we talked, he stopped taking notes about five minutes in. Somehow I was able to engage him, and he opened up to me. We actually had a wonderful conversation about his upbringing and his use history.

Amy told me later that this was an incredible instinct of mine, to refrain from trying to get people to change, but rather to meet them wherever they were. She said most counselors would have tried to shut him down, refusing to do the assessment if he was going to come in with that attitude. That never actually occurred to me.

The Alcohol and Other Drug Office was located in the student health center along the east side of campus, along with doctors' offices, a psychiatry clinic, and a pharmacy. I was a frequent user of the student health center and had formed a relationship with one of the primary care doctors there. I manipulated her into prescribing 30 Lortabs (double strength Vicodin) for me every three months for what I identified as chronic headaches. I deftly used my status at the alcohol and other drug office as cover—counting on her to think *clearly I could not work there if I had a problem*—and I was using the opioid for true medical pain. It was an effective cover.

In the beginning, the prescription would last the full three months. They were especially enjoyed every few days in combination with a food binge. But over a couple of years, I began to use them daily. I started blowing through the 30 pills in two weeks. I knew it would be suspicious to ask for more, so I always bided my time until the three months were up, and then requested a new prescription.

Simultaneously, I was active in several recovery programs: Overeaters Anonymous, CoDependents Anonymous (CoDA, a 12-step program for people with relationship issues), and Al-Anon (a program for loved ones of people with substance use disorders.) I attended three to four meetings a week. I was not honest about my use in any of these meetings.

Over the next several years, while I was hiding my growing pill addiction, I became a superstar student on the outside. I continued to work in the Alcohol and Other Drug Office, developing my expertise in substance use. Lauded by my professors for my intelligence and hard work, I launched and co-led a group for students wanting support in finishing their theses and dissertations. I even won a prestigious award for graduate students in my division of the American Psychological Association.

In the final year of my training, it was time to complete my one-year internship, a requirement for all students getting a doctorate in psychology. This meant leaving the school for full-time training at some psychological services site in the country. I applied to 13 sites and received 11 interviews, perhaps the highest ratio of my cohort. This was a huge improvement from the previous lukewarm response to my graduate school applications. I ended up matching with my first choice spot at Duke University, another great honor. All of this while I was using and bingeing daily.

During this time, I started dating Chris. It was a whirlwind romance, and within six months, we were looking for a house to buy. I had never experienced restful sleep in my life, and having a regular bedmate really brought these difficulties to the forefront. So I was assessed at the local sleep clinic and diagnosed with four sleep disorders: obstructive sleep apnea, restless legs syndrome, delayed sleep phase disorder, and periodic limb movements in sleep. I started using a CPAP machine and was prescribed a nightly Ambien to help regulate my sleep cycle and calm my body. And for a couple of years, I used it as directed.

When I was living in Durham, North Carolina, during my internship, I drove six hours one day—through an afternoon and evening—to visit my mother in Atlanta. The long drive was fueled by much Mt. Dew and nicotine. Upon arrival late that night, I was wired. So I decided to take two Ambien to counteract the effects of the drive and stimulants. This triggered my first ever blackout.

I awoke the next morning and became aware that at a certain point, I had no memory of the previous night, after taking the Ambien. I knew Ambien sometimes had this side effect, and it alarmed me to have experienced it. At the same time, I felt drawn to the sleepy, hypnotic feeling that two Ambien brought me.

After I returned home to North Carolina, I added occasional abuse of this medication to my abuse of the Lortabs. One morning, I woke up to find a lottery ticket and a pack of cigarettes on the kitchen counter. I deduced that sometime the night prior, I had driven in this blackout to a local gas station and bought both. I had absolutely no memory of the event. This time, my alarm meter blared.

When I had moved to Durham, I continued my 12-step involvement and joined local CoDA and Al-Anon meetings. I also discovered there was a gay AA meeting on the Duke campus. There had been no gay meetings in Champaign-Urbana. I wanted to meet other gay people in recovery, so although I didn't really drink, I began attending this meeting. I liked this group, so I lied and presented myself as someone who was in recovery from alcohol and drugs, with significant clean time. At one point, I even "confessed" a slip, and had to reset my clean time, assuaging the guilt and shame I felt over hiding my ongoing use.

Over the course of that internship year, my relationship with Chris fell apart. Two days after we officially called it quits, I received the phone call from Hazelden offering me their postdoctoral fellowship. Amy and I had charted my course years ago, and given their incredible reputation, this was a dream come true. I had originally wanted to do my pre-doctoral internship at Hazelden, but Amy said it would be better for me to intern at a college counseling center that had a multicultural focus. She felt this could give me good generalist training, and then I could do a postdoc at Hazelden to specialize in addiction psychology. So that's what I did.

I didn't realize it was so rare to get a postdoc at Hazelden. They almost always filled their postdocs internally from their interns, but about once every five years, they had an opening that could go to an outside person. As luck would have it, this happened during my year.

But back to the blackout . . .

I had received the Hazelden offer and needed to officially accept it. But there was one problem: it included signing a statement that I didn't have any active substance use problems. In the state of Minnesota, where Hazelden is located, a law at the time stated that you must be "free from chemical use problems" for two years to work in a treatment center.

I took the statement to my therapist to process. I'd been open with her all along about how much I was using. As I sat with the statement in my hands, contemplating committing perjury, she looked at me with incredible concern. Then she leaned forward and put her hand on my arm.

"What are you going to do?" she gently asked.

"I'm going to sign the paper," I answered, quietly but resolutely. "I have to. This offer is too much to pass up, and besides, I have nowhere else to go." My relationship with Chris had just ended. I literally had nothing left in Illinois to go back to.

The therapist leaned back and locked eyes with me, trying to decide how best to challenge me.

"How do you think this is going to end?" she asked softly.

"I don't know," I said. "I don't know. . . ."

We sat in silence for some time, both considering that question.

At that point in time, I knew I'd abused prescription pills, but I felt I was far more active in my eating disorder. Maybe I thought I still had control, and that I would stop using before I got to Hazelden, thereby justifying my false attestation.

Denial is a wicked beast.

The truth is, when I was admitted to Hazelden's postdoctoral training program, I was thrilled. I felt I was going to get to be a part of something special. I was also incredibly intimidated and scared. All my supervisors had given me feedback that I was a very good therapist, but this definitely felt like several levels up from what I had been doing. Would I be good here?

When I arrived at the main campus for my first day of orientation, a family of deer literally scampered in front of me as I drove up the winding driveway. *Where am I?* I wondered wide-eyed, feeling incredibly lucky to be joining such a tradition.

After two weeks of orientation, I settled into my postdoc routine. I worked two days a week in the St. Paul outpatient facility, providing assessments and therapy to adults, and three days a week in the Plymouth residential facility, where I worked with adolescents and young adults receiving inpatient care. All my supervisors continued to reflect positive feedback regarding my work.

As had happened when I first started working at the university alcohol and other drug office five years prior, I felt myself coming alive again in my role. Even now I tell students: put me in a room with a surly adolescent, and I'm in heaven. I just get them. I quickly took over the one of the therapy groups, which taught emotional and interpersonal coping skills to patients with these identified problems. I also facilitated the LGBTQ+ group, where I got to utilize all the things I had learned as a graduate student when I specialized in this population. Because I was not yet licensed, I worked under supervision from a senior psychologist.

I *loved* being a part of a treatment team. Our team held weekly staffings, where all the providers talked about each of the patients, each contributing their particular expertise. I found that most of the people working there were just as driven and passionate as I was. I truly felt lucky to be a part of such an organization. The months passed, and I continued to do well. But working in a residential treatment center for substance use disorders heightened the yo-yo experience of becoming a gifted practitioner on the one hand, and a spiraling addict on the other.

I meanwhile joined a gay Narcotics Anonymous group and became active in the Minnesota recovery community. I talked at meetings about my false sobriety, I shared my false story, I went out for fellowship every week, and I answered 12-step calls. As my situation got more and more out of hand, I began to feel more and more depressed. I was not being honest anywhere— with anyone—anymore. I would go to work high, only to receive a heartfelt note from a client telling me how helpful and inspiring I had been to them. I felt trapped but had no idea of how to get out of the mess.

There's a line in one of the introductory readings at Narcotics Anonymous that haunted me—"We are people in the grip of a continuing and progressive illness whose ends are always the same: jails, institutions, and death." At every meeting when this was read, I thought back to the question my therapist asked, and realized I had my answer. How was this going to end? Each time the statement was read, I recognized that I was either going to jail or a mental institution, or I would die by suicide or overdose. I wanted desperately to get sober, but had zero desire to be sober. And so I got up each day, swallowed handfuls of pills, fulfilled the role of the imposter addiction mental health professional, talked the recovery game at meetings, and waited in despair for the inevitable: jail, institution, or death.

As it turns out, all three came knocking on my door.

Healing 6

Hazelden Betty Ford

You can't be in recovery and not hear about Hazelden Betty Ford. Their reputation in the field is undisputable. They are often ranked as the nation's top addiction treatment provider. A lot of people have heard of their treatment center, especially since famous people go there—but they also have a large publishing arm, which produces a great deal of the recovery literature in the field. They create curriculums for treatment centers, videos with lectures, and structured workbooks and the like, which form the top curriculum used by treatment centers, schools, and prisons in the United States. Their daily meditation books are read from to open or close thousands of 12-step meetings all across the world every day. In short, you can't get through most 12-step meetings, or a day in treatment anywhere, without being touched by Hazelden Betty Ford in some way.

But Hazelden Betty Ford is so much more than that. It's talked about with pure reverence and awe by people in recovery who utilize 12-step programs. Strike up a conversation with truckers in recovery at a truck stop in Arkansas, and Hazelden will be given a special, vaulted place. Have a conversation with a group of doctors in recovery in New York, and Hazelden will be credited with saving someone's life. It is truly that impactful. Their renewal center offers various weekend retreats that people make vacations out of, covering dozens of recovery topics. The main campus is commonly referred to as the "Shangri-La" of recovery places. People frequently talk about making "pilgrimages" there. For real.

There's even a book published on the history of the organization. Read it, and you'll learn that Hazelden started as non-profit treatment center in 1949 for professional men, out in a farmhouse north of the Twin Cities in Minnesota. It expanded its treatment to women in 1956, and youth in 1981. They started a counselor training program in 1963, which remains the oldest continuous addiction counselor training education program in the US. This evolved into the Hazelden Graduate School of Addiction Studies in 1999, and is where I work today.

Hazelden pioneered a multidisciplinary treatment called the Minnesota Model, which brought together a team of professionals, including doctors, nurses, psychologists, and counselors, each contributing their expertise to the patient's care. They highlighted the need to treat each client with dignity and respect, which was sorely lacking in most treatment in those days. They've developed specialized treatment programs for health care professionals and lawyers. They merged with the Betty Ford Center in 2014, and are now called Hazelden Betty Ford.

Their main location is in Center City, Minnesota, on a bucolic 217 acres. It borders a lake, and several trails wind for miles around the property. They also have three outpatient locations in the Twin Cities, and a youth treatment center just west of the Cities. Hazelden Betty Ford also has other treatment locations in California, Oregon, Washington, Chicago, Florida, and New York. They run a family program and a children's program. It has a center for research and runs a week-long immersion experience for doctors and professionals to learn about addiction and its treatment. Its CEO has testified before Congress, advocating for policy changes to support people with substance use disorders. They recently started focusing on prevention work in schools. In short, anywhere addiction is, you will find Hazelden Betty Ford.

Among substance use treatment professionals, Hazelden Betty Ford is also held in special regard. It is regarded as the best: the best treatment center, the best treatment materials, the best training school. It sets the standard for the profession. Many have a lifelong ambition to work for the organization, and getting a job there is considered reaching a pinnacle of one's profession. It's often referred to as the Harvard of treatment centers. It continues to use a 12-Step approach, but also utilizes other evidence-based practices, like cognitive behavioral therapy, motivational interviewing, and medications for addiction treatment. Hazelden Betty Ford has helped hundreds of thousands of people recover.

Hazelden Betty Ford's dominance and standards lie in stark contrast to much of the recovery industry. For many individual and systemic reasons, the landscape of recovery centers in America is littered with opportunistic, unethical practices. Families desperate to get help for their loved ones are often taken advantage of, and patients of these treatment centers are strung along to maximize insurance payments to the facility.

We have a lot to do as an industry to clean up the field. Hazelden Betty Ford provides a trustworthy gold standard for many who are rightfully wary of getting help. Families should follow published guidelines to vet any treatment center before sending a loved one there. There are many such guides available online.

Healing 7

Emotions 101

Most clients coming into therapy have some difficulty identifying their emotions. That's part of the reason they're coming to see us. Many therapists have feelings charts that outline different emotions, with cartoon faces to express a variety of emotions. The most popular chart has 30 different emotions. Therapists often whip these out during a session with a client who is trying to identify what they're feeling. Feelings work is a big part of what we do.

But I have found some people have extreme difficulty identifying an emotion even when they are presented with a chart like this. Moreover, most of my clients have not been taught what emotions are, why they feel them, or how to use them. So over the years, I developed a crash course on emotions to explain what and how emotions work, which I call Emotions 101.

Here's the lesson I share . . .

There are four basic emotion groups: mad, sad, glad, and scared. There are a couple of others (surprise, disgust), but for the most part, every emotion is a form or mixture of mad, sad, glad, or scared. Frustrated? That's mad. Apprehensive? That's scared. Lonely? That's sad. Silly? That's glad.

Emotions are critical to our existence. We evolved to feel emotions in order to process events in our lives. Our emotions have become like an additional sense, joining sight, smell, and the others. But they come from within us as we make sense of our environment, instead of from outside of us. Our emotions are meant to guide our responses, to keep us safe and prosperous.

Each emotion cues us into a different event that has happened, so we can figure out how to respond as an organism. We feel scared when there is a real or a perceived threat. We feel mad when there is a real or perceived injustice. We feel sad when there is a real or perceived loss. And we feel glad when all our basic needs are met. In this way, there are no "bad" emotions. All emotions are good.

When emotions are working the way they evolved, we are then supposed to take this information and respond. When I feel there's a threat, I do things to try to feel safe, or get away from the source of the threat. When I feel there's a loss, I understand that I need to grieve letting go of something that meant something to me. When I feel there's an injustice, my anger gives me a boost of energy to help fight for my or someone else's rights. And when I feel glad, I can express gratitude for being satisfied, content, or connected, and do more of what it took to get there.

However, feeling emotions can sometimes involve some detective work. Whenever we feel a so-called negative emotion, we first need to identify the threat, injustice, or loss behind the feeling. This will help us figure out what part of our environment we need to respond to. If I'm feeling scared about an upcoming trip, maybe it's because I'm feeling that my life might be threatened by traveling on a plane. If I'm feeling sad about leaving a job, then I'm probably feeling a loss of something meaningful. *Then, and this is critical, once we've identified that correlation, we must determine if the threat, injustice, or loss is real, or just perceived.*

Many of our emotional reactions are due to skewed interpretations of reality. The system that evolved our emotions also evolved an over-tendency to identify threats or injustices. Evolutionarily, it helped our species survive to do this. The caveman who jumped at his own shadow never saw any harm, but the one who failed to jump at the sight of a saber-toothed tiger did. Not every perceived threat is a danger to us, but in evolutionary terms, it's better to react to everything then under-react when it counts.

If this is the case, we can identify our false belief and work to better align it with reality. For example, if I feel fear about flying in a plane, I can recognize that this as a perception, given the incredibly low chances of dying in a plane crash. Therefore, I can engage in mental and physical strategies to calm the overreaction in my body.

If the threat, injustice, or loss is real, we can then identify a plan to respond to gain safety, rectify an injustice, or grieve a loss. For example, if I'm sad about leaving a job, I can justify this as a real feeling and say goodbye to my cowork-ers or somehow otherwise mark the transition, thereby engaging in an active grief process.

I use this lesson with clients who grew up in homes that didn't teach them what emotions are, how they are meant to help us, and how to respond to them. Many of my clients come in with the belief that mad, sad, and scared are "bad emotions" and should be avoided. This is what their families and social groups have taught them. Or some come in having been taught that angry and happy are the only two acceptable emotions. To the contrary, I say, all emotions are very important, and we should seek to move toward them, with curiosity, and explore.

Sometimes it takes a few months for clients to progress through Emotions 101. I give them homework to write down a feeling, categorize it, and name the underlying trigger. We then work to separate out real or perceived, and discuss all the options the person has for their response. I teach clients that we never have to sit in or suppress any emotion; in fact, sitting in or suppressing an emotion will only compound its expression, since our bodies tend to "shout" the emotion louder when we aren't responding to it.

I teach my counseling students, too, how to work with their clients and deliver Emotions 101. Funnily enough, many of my students have never had emotional instruction themselves and find it very helpful for their own lives! It's funny, sometimes, how counselors often benefit personally from their education. I'll say, this lesson about emotions is definitely one of the most important I've learned in my life.

Wounded 5

Cover

About nine months into my postdoctoral fellowship, things were really humming along. Then I experienced a week which captured the wounded and healing threads of my life perfectly.

Even though I was on a postdoctoral fellowship, I actually wasn't a doctor yet. Part of completing a doctoral degree in psychology includes writing an in-depth research paper called a dissertation. It typically involves years of work, first exploring the scientific literature to situate a new study in it, then designing that study, collecting data from research participants, analyzing it, writing up the results, and defending it before a panel of experts. Most people with doctorates describe their dissertation as the hardest part of getting their degree. It certainly was for me.

All students are encouraged to wrap up their dissertations before they start—or certainly by the time they complete—their internships. But I fell into an unfortunate group of people who wasn't able to do this. I was accepted into my postdoc with the agreement that I would complete it ASAP.

The trouble I was having in completing it wasn't academic, or time management, or resource management. It was psychological. I actually enjoyed designing the study and collecting the data, and could even spend hours analyzing the data with complicated statistics. But writing up the results nearly killed me. I had actively avoided this part, because writing was such a painful process for me. I just hated writing. I could never spend more than an hour at a time sitting at the computer for this part of the project.

I didn't figure all this out until much later, but it turns out that every time I sat down to write, I was subconsciously imagining a critical person standing behind me, reading every word and phrase, clucking their tongues, and commenting that what I wrote was trash. In short, writing was a shame-based experience for me. No wonder I avoided it. I seriously considered chucking my whole degree, because I didn't think I could do it. That would have meant throwing away eight years of dedicated study because of one paper. Yes, writing was that painful.

Once I started my fellowship, I made a deal with myself. I would commit to writing 1.5 hours per night after work, and 10 hours a weekend, for three months. If I couldn't get it done in this time, I would accept that and move on to a different career.

And so I wrote. Having a definitive end date to the torture was the only thing that helped. Lo and behold, I was able to finish the manuscript and send it off to my committee. It wasn't perfect by a long shot, but it was good enough. I defended it before my committee, and after nine long years, I was approved to graduate.

Graduation was Mother's Day weekend. My family flew from across the country to attend, and watch as I walked across the stage and got hooded by two of my mentors. I couldn't believe it. After a decade of self-doubt and setbacks, it had finally happened. I was officially a doctor. It was the biggest accomplishment of my life.

I returned to Minneapolis with my newly minted title. Two days later, one of the social workers on our team unexpectedly quit. My manager had to scramble to figure something out. She asked to meet with me, and offered me a full-time job. I still had three months left on my fellowship, so this was a great vote of confidence in my abilities. When she told me what the salary was, I nearly gagged. It was almost twice what I was making as a training fellow! After a decade in student poverty, I was going to be able to afford nice things. I accepted.

I couldn't believe my luck. I was still riding the wave of graduation celebration, and this just lifted it into tsunami status. This was turning into the best week of my life.

I was off from work that Friday. I thought it would be fun to go shopping, charge a few things to a credit card that I now knew I'd be able to pay off. God knows I hadn't had that feeling in years. And I thought a great way to reward myself for all these accomplishments was to go shopping high. I took a couple of Ambien and set off.

As the Ambien took hold, that dreamy, warm comfort settled in around me. By this time, I had converted Ambien from a sleeping medication to an anxiety medication. It no longer put me to sleep, but rather, relaxed me. I didn't, however, compute the dangers of driving on the drug.

At one point in my shopping, I needed to stop for gas. I pulled into the gas station and misjudged the curb. Due to the effects of the Ambien, I put too much pressure on the gas and hit the curb in just such a way that the front airbags suddenly went off. I was jolted. And deeply surprised. I didn't think

I'd come in that forcefully. I rolled the car back from the curb and got out to take in the damage. There appeared to be no outside damage to the car.

A gas station worker saw what happened and came out. She approached me.

"Are you okay?" she asked, showing her genuine concern and confusion.

I shot back an innocent defense: "I have no idea what happened; I just seemed to hit the curb at a weird angle; I was distracted for just a minute." I wasn't sure if the police were going to need to be called or not. My airbags had gone off. "Can I even drive the car in this state?" I then asked the attendant, trying to sound as innocent as possible.

I could tell the attendant didn't buy any of my act. She knew I was under the influence of something. Yet at the same time, she seemed to be on my side.

"You should probably get out of here before anyone is called," she said, surmising my state and the logical next events if I were to stay.

I sensed it was better to just follow her direction than to try and play out any accident scene. So I got in the car and drove the few blocks back to my apartment, then parked my car in the garage and went inside. I sat down in the living room and put my head in my hands. *What did I just do? How am I going to get out of this?*

After the shock had worn off, I opened my computer and started researching. There was no economical way to repair the airbags; the car was considered totaled. Fueled by an epic shame spiral, I then searched frantically at local dealerships for a used car. I located something quickly, called, and arranged to purchase it the next morning. By 10 a.m. on Saturday I left the dealership in my new car—problem solved, or so it seemed.

I covered my tracks by linking this purchase to all my good fortune from earlier in the week. I posted on Facebook that in the course of a week, I had graduated, been offered a new job, and bought a new car. The congratulations poured in. No one knew what was really happening.

Later I'd realize something: that this one week came to symbolize my whole addiction. I was achieving great things in my life, but underneath I was hiding a seething boil of inescapable turmoil. Still, I was managing to cover up those actions—even if the lid was threatening to blow off.

Healing 8

The Next Right Thing

One thing anyone new to 12-step recovery can see is the preponderance of sayings. Twelve-step recovery has a saying for every situation. *Progress not perfection. Keep coming back. It works if you work it. Keep it simple. One day at a time. Easy does it.* They're often written in bold font on posters plastered all over meeting rooms. They're meant to break down the complexities of recovery into easier, more manageable bits. Many of these sayings have crossed over into mainstream culture.

Most of these made sense to me. They were self-explanatory and easy to follow. But one really stumped me: *just do the next right thing.* Every time I heard this, I thought, *How in the hell do you know what the next right thing is?* I found it more confusing than helpful. In my experience, most of the time what felt right to me was just my addiction talking. The next right thing was to take another pill so I could feel better or avoid withdrawal, or tell another lie so I could preserve my job or get out of trouble.

One day back in graduate school I asked my clinical supervisor, Amy, who is also in recovery, about this.

"How do you figure out what the next right thing is?" I asked.

She smiled, and responded, "You know, that's not the full phrase."

"It's not? What's the full phrase?"

"The full phrase is: 'just do the next *right* thing, the next *loving* thing (you first), the next *courageous* thing.'"

My life seemed to change when I heard that. Ever since then, when trying to figure out what the next right thing to do or say is, I will ask myself, *Is what I'm about to do loving? Does it put loving myself first? Does it take courage?* If I can answer yes to these three questions, then I know it's the next right thing. Now it's my favorite saying.

Years later, I decided to research the origin of the phrase. I wanted to know who first explicated the *right thing* as the *next loving, courageous thing*. Turns out, there is no source that says what Amy told me. The phrase has sometimes been linked to the writings of Carl Jung, who said the best way to live life was to do the next right thing "with diligence and devotion." Even if I can't substantiate exactly where it came from, I like what Amy told me better. And it's the message I spread to students, clients, friends, and family whenever I can.

Healing 9

Three Lessons of Mistakes

I was raised to be a perfectionist. Many women are. As a perfectionist, mistakes used to be my mortal enemy. If I got a 99 on an assignment, I focused on the one point I missed. If I mispronounced a word during a class, it would haunt me for days. If I took a wrong turn in the directions, I sat down at the computer later to learn the correct route. Mistakes were to be avoided at all costs. I thought perfectionism was something to be strived for, the ultimate goal.

I've come to learn that perfectionism is actually toxic. In reality, it causes a lot of damage. This is because the root of this obsession is shame. Shame drives all perfection. Here's the logic: *If I am perfect, no one can find fault with me. I won't have to feel bad about myself. That feeling of being less than, of being worthless, of being unlovable would go away.*

This is in contrast to the healthy striving for excellence, which involves only putting in my best effort and accepting that I fall short sometimes. In this state of mind, it's okay to make mistakes. In perfectionism, mistakes only serve to reinforce the belief that I am not good enough.

The work I've had to do on letting go of perfectionism has gone on for decades. I still have to do this work today—learning to be okay with making mistakes. As I've done this work, my relationship with mistakes has evolved over time. The bulk of this change came to me in the following three lessons.

Lesson One

My first lesson came in eighth grade. I was absent one day for some reason, and the next day there was a pop quiz on what had happened the day before. I was not excused from the test and guessed at the answers. One of the questions was, "What color is the C string on the harp?" I had no clue that harps even had colored strings! Not surprisingly, I got the answer wrong. And because I got it wrong, I will know for the rest of my life that the color of the C string is red.

I think about this mistake often. I realize that if I had guessed right, I would never have retained that knowledge. My learning was facilitated by the mistake. The mistake was the reason I knew something. I came to see that sometimes our mistakes are our greatest teachers.

Lesson Two

I love the theory of evolution. I marvel at its beauty. I am in awe of its simplicity. One day in my 30s, I was sitting around, thinking about evolution (I recognize this isn't a typical activity!). I thought about how evolution actually happens. All life consists of DNA. DNA is the "blueprint" that tells the plant or animal how to make proteins and different cells, and everything else life needs to exist. DNA consists of two strands, spiraled together in a double helix that looks like a twisted ladder. The two strands are complementary. DNA has four base compounds: adenine (A), cytosine (C), guanine (G), and thymine (T). Adenine always pairs with thymine, and cytosine always pairs with guanine, forming A-T and C-G rungs in the ladder. When a cell goes to replicate, it splits the ladder in half, and then builds two new strands using the complementary base pair. But, every now and then, a mistake is made in the A-T and C-G pairing, producing a slightly different daughter cell. This is called a mutation. And sometimes, the mutation conveys some benefit to the organism. It might improve its chances for survival, or lead to more reproduction. It is only in this way that species develop and evolve.

And it hit me. We are *programmed,* at a cellular level, to make mistakes. And not only are mistakes okay, they are *necessary*. If transcription mistakes didn't happen, the human species wouldn't exist. No life would exist but the first prototypical single-celled organisms. I sat with this knowledge for a few minutes. *I exist because of mistakes. We all do. Mistakes are what allow change, and therefore improvement, to happen.*

Lesson Three

Sometime in graduate school, I was exposed to the concept of *wabi sabi*—a Japanese artistic aesthetic that delights in objects that are imperfect, unfinished, or unlasting. So the vase that has a crack in it is more beautiful, and therefore more perfect, than the unblemished vase. And the wooden bowl that's worn from years of use is more perfect than the brand new, never used bowl.

I found myself drawn to learning more. I wanted to be mindful of cultural appropriation and sought to explore this concept respectfully. I read a great deal about the concept and talked to some fellow students who hailed from Asia. The more I read about *wabi sabi,* the more I realized this is how I wanted to feel about people. I wanted to see the beauty in people for being imperfect. I wanted to feel connection with others on our shared impermanence. Over time, I have come to believe that people are beautiful not despite of, but because of, their mistakes.

This last lesson has had the greatest impact on me. Even though I could recognize that mistakes could be great teachers—and that all of life depended on mistakes—mistakes still felt somehow wrong. But ever since I took *wabi sabi* to heart, I started celebrating mistakes. When I realized I had made a mistake, I didn't automatically shame myself. I would pause and feel a sense of beauty, thinking, *I have just been reminded that I am human, and I feel connected to the human experience.* These days, whenever I make a mistake, I think to myself, *Huh, there I go, being beautiful.*

Wounded 6

Addicted Addiction Psychologist

A few months after I landed the full-time job (and once I had reliable health insurance), I decided to seek gastric bypass surgery. A family member had had it about five years prior, and it had been very successful for them. At that time, I was very anti-surgery. I knew their weight was a result of an eating disorder, and as I was developing a specialization in addiction psychology, I strongly felt that a surgical intervention was not the answer for a mental disorder. But it actually worked well for them; they had dropped a tremendous amount of weight and kept it off. Moreover, they began to engage in life more and were building a happy existence.

I definitely didn't have a happy existence. Despite six years in Overeaters Anonymous, I had actually gained weight. I began to consider the surgery as I became more desperate.

Living life in a larger body in our society is extremely difficult. For me, life in my body was a miserable existence. When I was a student, I was always the first one to class so I could try out the desks to find the one that I felt least uncomfortable in. I never wore pants because I hated how they accentuated my hanging belly. Travelling was an exercise in humiliation; I would have to ask the flight attendant for the seat-belt extension, and withstand eye-rolling huffs of disgust from my seatmates. Even basic personal hygiene needs were becoming difficult. I was totally mobile, but I could not put anything in my lap, because I had no lap. When I did assessments with clients, I had to use a small side table to write on. I was deeply ashamed. I *hated* my body.

I learned that there was a six-month pre-surgery screening and preparation process.

At the time, to qualify for bariatric surgery, a patient must have a body mass index (BMI) above 40, or above 35 if they had a complicating health condition. My BMI was 56.2; I weighed 320 pounds, so I clearly qualified there.

Throughout the process, a number of physical and psychological tests must be passed, designed to rule out any people with medical or mental health problems that would be contraindicative of success after the surgery. For example, people with active eating disorders are ruled out. So are people with active substance use disorders.

In these assessments, I acknowledged a previous eating disorder, but hid my current binge eating behaviors. I had to document a timeline of all my efforts to lose weight over two decades, and the results of those efforts. I had to work with their clinicians for six months, making behavioral changes to prove that my weight was resistant to behavioral interventions.

In all the psychological assessments for the surgery—and there were many—I lied about my problems with substances. My scores on a standardized personality assessment came back invalid, indicating I was being evasive. My psychologist interpreted this as being due to the fact that I was so familiar with the assessment, since I administered it to every one of my clients at Hazelden. I got approved for the surgery in December, and I scheduled it for the following Valentine's Day. I found the date significant. *It will be the ultimate gift of love to myself*, I thought.

The gastric bypass surgery itself reroutes food in the body. The surgeon takes the top of the stomach and creates a pouch, puts aside the rest of the stomach, and connects the pouch directly to a section of the small intestine. For a normal person, an empty stomach is about the size of your fist, but with a binge, can expand to hold up to four quarts of food. When fully recovered from surgery, this pouch holds about a cup of food. In this way, food "bypasses" the stomach and goes into the small intestine.

Because the surgery creates a route where the food enters further along the small intestine, this means the body misses some opportunity to digest the food, creating a system where less nutrients are absorbed. This requires the recipient to commit to lifelong consumption of a number of different vitamins. The whole system also changes gut hormones, causing the individual to feel fuller longer. Finally, it is hypothesized to change the body's set weight to be lower, allowing the individual to maintain less body weight.

My surgery required a six-week liquid fast, which was difficult, but I managed to follow it. The procedure went as expected, and my sisters came to care for me post-surgery.

It was another two months after the surgery before I could reintroduce solid food to my diet. Within three months, I had lost 60 pounds. Now it was time to start building that happy existence.

That May, I went on a solo vacation. I had three simple rules for the vacation: I would use no maps, stop when something looked interesting, eat when I was hungry, and find a place to sleep each night when I became tired.

I drove north, stopping at various attractions along the north shore of Minnesota. I crossed into Canada and ended up north of Thunder Bay. I passed by a billboard that advertised Canada's longest, highest, and fastest zip line adventure. I followed the signs there to Eagle Canyon.

It was early in the season and very few people were there. I had never zip-lined before, and thought that would make a great end to my adventure. I entered the trailer office and paid my fee.

The clerk announced, "This zip line had a limit of 280 pounds."

I announced back with a grin, "I am well below that at 250 pounds." I was thrilled. It was the first milestone in my weight recovery. Here was my happy existence coming to life.

For decades, I had not met the weight limit for anything. On more than one occasion, I suffered the humiliation of going to a roller coaster park with friends, only to be removed from a ride because I could not get the safety bar to lock in place because my belly was too big. Each time, my friends would avoid eye contact and say they were sorry. Each time, I'd have to meet them at the end of the ride. It was a full-on shame-spiral every time.

On several occasions during my internship and fellowship, my supervisor had to approach me to let me know that a client I'd been assigned was uncomfortable working with me because of my weight. The supervisor, too, would avoid eye contact and say they were sorry. Once, I thought about asking them if they would reassign a client who didn't like the race of their therapist. But the truth is, my shame over my weight was so great, I'm not sure I would have felt comfortable working with a client who felt that way about me.

I continued to lose weight over the next year after surgery, reaching a low of 200 pounds. I had to replace my entire closet—and discovered I got to have a fashion sense for the first time in 15 years. When you're as large as I was, fashion takes a back seat to *does-it-adequately-cover-my-body?* Most plus-size clothing stores only go up to size 28; I topped out at a size 36. This meant the only source of clothing for me had been online, where I was unable to try anything on, and pretty much had to take whatever I could find. But now I could now shop in local stores. I delighted that I could walk into a local store and browse all the clothes, getting to actually try them on and see if I liked them. I could even fit into the upper end of "normal" size clothing, which was beyond my wildest imagination. In many ways, I'd found a whole new world. Everyone around me noticed this new body emerging, and I was congratulated all around.

There was one pesky downside to getting the surgery: I could no longer eat my feelings. At this time, I could hold about a half cup of food in my stomach-pouch at a time. Foods high in fat or sugar produced a "dumping" response by my body, whereby I would feel awful for about an hour after eating. But I came up with a "solution": I compensated by relying more and more on the prescription pills that I had been abusing.

In the next few months, my substance use skyrocketed to compensate for my inability to binge on food. This was exactly what the screening process for the surgery was designed to rule out. I was intelligent and conniving enough to thwart the screening process, but not enough to outsmart my addiction.

Opioids had been my drug of choice ever since wisdom tooth surgery, but now they became essential for my existence. I adored the numb, oblivious feeling they delivered.

There is nothing worse than a smart addict. We excel in finding ways to get drugs. There is no system we can't figure out. There is no problem we can't solve. There are no situations we can't spin. There are no people we can't manipulate. We will always find a way.

Over several months, I was able to set up a system that used various doctors and pharmacies. I visited a bogus pain clinic to get a prescription. One particularly desperate afternoon, I purposely injured my hand with a hammer and went to urgent care, saying I was reaching for a cast iron frying pan from the top shelf and it fell on my resting hand.

Many times, I didn't get what I wanted. I sometimes was given less strong pain medications. But it didn't matter. All I needed was the prescriber's Drug Enforcement Administration (DEA) number, which was typically included on the written prescription. A DEA number is assigned to medical professionals, allowing them to write prescriptions for controlled substances. It must be included on each written prescription for any controlled substance that gets taken to the pharmacy.

Once I had the DEA number, I set about on my computer to recreate the prescription in a Word document. I had picked up a great talent for creating Word documents that mimicked posters and other things in all the temp jobs I'd worked in Chicago a decade earlier. Since most prescriptions were printed on plain paper, all I had to do was match the formatting and fonts of the original prescription, substituting my preferred drug in the Rx section. By this point, I had learned the correct way to write a prescription, noting amount, strength, frequency, route, and refills in correct shorthand language. I would print it off, forging the prescriber's signature.

In this way, I worked three different pharmacies and made sure I timed the prescriptions to make sense with my history. I would never try to fill a prescription early.

I knew this was a very illegal thing to do. Forging prescriptions is considered a class three or four felony that can result in a three- to five-year prison sentence, and/or up to a $10,000 fine. I knew I was gambling with my life to engage in such a practice.

I did all of this during the evenings and weekends off from helping people recover from their own addictions. I would leave work after leading a therapy group on coping with triggers and drive straight to the pharmacy to pick up my own forged prescription.

By this time, people were becoming more aware of the opioid epidemic in our country, and most states had created prescription monitoring programs to help identify people who were abusing the medical system. I knew that it would only take one pharmacist a couple of extra minutes to check the monitoring database for my name. If they did this, my life as I knew it would be over.

I managed this risk by writing prescriptions that were common for people with chronic pain. I would approach each pharmacy in a way that was inviting and non-threatening. I would indicate that I would wait for the prescription, knowing this created a social pressure that decreased the chance the pharmacist would check the state prescription monitoring program for my history of prescriptions. I'd engage in pleasant chit-chat with the workers, designed to manipulate them into liking me—hopefully swaying any question they might have. I also went at times when the pharmacy was busy, knowing this would decrease the likelihood that someone would have the extra few minutes to check. I never used my insurance to pay for any of the forged prescriptions; I always indicated I didn't have any insurance. I was also a White, middle-class female; this alone allotted me a certain amount of privilege.

But every time, I knew I was gambling with my life. I would always walk into the pharmacy with a heightened awareness that today could be the day I got caught. I would sit in the pharmacy waiting area and observe the pharmacist out of the corner of my eye. Sometimes, I would see them pick up the phone, and I would wonder if this was it. *Are they calling in my fraud to bust me?* I would hold my breath, waiting for the inevitable arrival of the police. Flashes of being arrested, losing my career, becoming a laughingstock in my field passed through my mind. My heart would thump in my chest; my breathing would be shallow and quick. Calm yourself, I'd say, you must look like you are pleasantly waiting with nothing to hide.

I never got caught. I maintained this system for about nine months, obtaining massive amounts of opioids every month. Most prescriptions for opioids are meant to be taken four times a day, for a total of 28 a week. I typically went through 120 double-strength Vicodin during this timeframe, or 240 regular strength doses. Every morning, I rolled out of bed and started to build that day's high by immediately popping two pills. I'd learned that a really good high had to be built in layers, over time. Those two pills would build the base, and then I'd add another pill every hour until I reached maximum oblivion. Once I reached this state, I maintained it by taking additional pills less frequently.

All of this was taking place as I was moving forward in my career as an addiction psychologist. In the year since I'd been hired full-time, I was seen as a talented, rising star. I was the main mental health provider for part of a unit. But I also provided mental health assessments and coverage for the rest of the facility, in addition to providing individual outpatient therapy to adolescents and adults. I was routinely receiving cards and comments by patients and coworkers alike saying that I was a gifted provider. One time a card said, "I can't thank you enough for what you've meant to me. At a time where I felt like everything was falling apart, you helped me put some things back together and make something new. You have touched my life and made such a huge impact."

I was also working my way through the requirements to obtain my license as a psychologist in the state of Minnesota. This was not an easy task. It required one year of supervised practice (minimum 1,800 hours), passing a difficult psychology exam in addition to a state ethics exam, and submitting two letters of endorsement by licensed psychologists.

The exam is called the EPPP (pronounced "E-triple P"), or the Examination for Professional Practice in Psychology. It is a 225-question, four-hour exam that covers eight content areas meant to represent all the basic knowledge every psychologist should have.

Most people I knew spent several months with dedicated study in order to prepare for the exam. I blocked off three months myself, and studied about 20 hours a week. I took the exam in November. I was on the end of a self-created opioid taper so that I could take the exam without having to be loaded. I wasn't sure how I performed. I knew many people who failed the exam the first time. I sat on pins and needles for two weeks waiting for the results. If I passed, I still had to pass the state ethics exam. Then I had submit my full application for review by the Board of Psychology.

How I was able to do all of this while taking all the drugs I was using baffles me to this day. This was a period of intense development of my career, yet I was able to excel at work while taking handfuls of pills each day. But all of this was about to change in a big way.

Healing 10

Shame Disorder

There's a guide that most mental health practitioners use to diagnose patients. It's called the Diagnostic and Statistical Manual of Mental Disorders (DSM) and is published by the American Psychiatric Association. It organizes all the recognized mental health disorders into groups and gives descriptions of the symptoms of each disorder, as well as other pertinent information like prevalence, course, and a description of other disorders that each one is sometimes confused with. The DSM currently includes 157 disorders organized into 20 groups.

As a counselor educator, I spend a lot of time teaching students what's in the manual and how to use it. And there are many problems with the DSM, but it's the system we currently use in medical care. One of the biggest problems with the manual is that it largely identifies problems as residing within the individual (a person *has* anxiety, or depression, or OCD), while ignoring that many of our problems reside within our environment (such as reactions to oppression or lack of social support).

Over the years, I've been given many different diagnoses from this manual. I've been diagnosed with major depressive disorder, bulimia, generalized anxiety disorder, body dysmorphia, persistent depressive disorder, binge eating disorder, bipolar II disorder, opioid use disorder, PTSD, and several others.

While I had symptoms of most of these disorders, none of them adequately described my mental health picture. Every time I met with a new therapist or psychiatrist, they would review my list of symptoms and do their best to hang the most correct labels on me. But most acknowledged that I didn't fit neatly into any of the options in the DSM.

I've come to believe I wasn't really suffering from any of these disorders. All my problems, and all my symptoms, were connected to *shame*. So I decided to create a new mental health disorder, called *shame disorder,* and developed a list of diagnostic criteria for it in the language and format of the DSM.

Shame Disorder

Diagnostic Criteria

A. Excessive feelings of shame, occurring more days than not, for at least six months. Shame is characterized by at least three of the following:

1. Deeply held beliefs that the individual has little worth

2. Feelings of self-hatred

3. Excessive feelings of embarrassment or humiliation when the individual makes a mistake

4. The individual attributes any success to luck and never to personal ability

5. Beliefs that one's body is unattractive or somehow ugly

B. The individual has a running internal dialogue that labels almost all their actions and interactions as incorrect, deficient, or otherwise not good enough

C. The individual has difficulty forming and maintaining intimate relationships

D. The individual attempts to cope with the shame by at least two of the following:

1. Withdrawing from close personal relationships

2. Excessive use of substances or behaviors in an attempt to numb one's feelings, including alcohol, opiates, sedative/hypnotics, eating, shopping, compulsive sex, gaming

3. Adopting a perfectionistic approach to life

4. The development of a hyper-confident persona

E. The shame causes clinically significant distress or impairment in social, occupational, or other important areas of functioning

F. The disturbance is not attributable to the physiological effects of a substance or medication or another medical condition.

My shame developed early, in my childhood, for sure.

It's common for children to develop an imaginary friend. I hazily remember that as a child, I believed that I had an imaginary identical twin. Except one of us was born evil, and the other one was born good. The adults determined that it would be best to kill the evil baby. Except that they mistakenly killed the wrong twin. I, the evil one, had survived, but nobody knew they had made a mistake, so I had to pretend to be the good twin.

I never voiced this belief with anyone, but it definitely describes how I felt most of my childhood. If that's not a shame-based personality, I don't know what is.

It turns out when I look at my life from this shame lens, everything I did makes sense. The family I grew up in was shame-based, so this worldview was passed down to me. It was strengthened and cemented by the social trauma and rejection I experienced in eighth grade. I literally got messages every day that I was no good, and had no worth. This helped explain the explosion of my eating disorder in high school. As my body grew, it garnered judgment from other people, which I internalized. Shame also helped explain the depression I carried throughout most of my life. It explained all of my suicide attempts. My crippling social and situational anxiety were definitely a result of feeling shame. And this shame certainly explained my addiction to pills. Every pill I took was an attempt to shut off the pervasive shame I felt and deliver me to a place of numbness and oblivion. Of course, my using behavior only generated more shame, creating a self-perpetuating cycle.

All my mental health symptoms can be attributed to shame in some way. Part of what I desperately needed was a shame treatment program.

We didn't talk much about shame in my doctoral program. I don't remember addressing it with any of the clients I worked with on any of my clinical placements. We would frequently focus on self-esteem, but this is a different focus.

Then two seminal people came along and upended all of this in the course of a decade. The first is Dr. Kristen Neff, who studies something she called *self-compassion*. She helped me understand that self-esteem is how we feel about ourselves when we do good, but self-compassion is how we feel when we fall short. Her work was groundbreaking. She began publishing on it in 2003, and as part of her work, developed a layperson-focused website that described the concept and how to address low self-compassion. The other groundbreaker was Dr. Brene Brown, who brought her academic work on shame and vulnerability to the public in 2010. She's a researcher who defied the tenets of her social work profession by studying such a negative experience, and as a result, has helped millions of people in their journey to recover from shame. Both have helped me tremendously.

It was only when I focused all of my healing work on shame that I began to recover from all the diagnoses I had been given.

One time, when I was just a year or so sober, I confessed to my therapist that I had taken an oil change coupon that was addressed to my girlfriend Sarah. It was just for a few dollars off, but I wanted it, so I stole it. I told my therapist about it as evidence that I was really a bad person. I couldn't get over my shame over stealing this from someone I loved.

My therapist, bless her heart, tried her best to get me to see that what I had done was not reprehensible. She even disclosed that it was something that she might have done, and that it wasn't a big deal.

I spent a good four weeks of therapy fixated on this event. That's 200 minutes hyper-focused on a three-dollar coupon. But nothing my therapist said worked to get me to see that I didn't need to beat myself up over this, or that it wasn't proof that I was a bad person.

Exhausted, my therapist decided to try a different tack. She leaned back in her chair and looked me in the eyes with admiration.

"You're a person of great integrity," she said confidently.

This stopped me in my tracks. A puzzled look came over my face. "How in the world could you say that?"

"Because," she explained, "this little thing caused you such anguish, and only a person with lots of integrity would be this bothered by it."

This shift was what finally got through to me. As we continued to talk, our focus changed from shame to integrity.

What was happening was that I was a person who had high values and standards for my behavior, and when I lived in a way that was not in line with this, I experienced shame. I had always thought that because I did bad things, this meant I had no values. That I was always only out for myself, and a liar and a thief. Hence, the stealing of the coupon showed that I was a low-life.

But what if this wasn't what was happening? What if I simply believed deeply in honesty and respect in my relationships and felt that taking the coupon broke these deeply held values? And what if this discordance is what generated my feeling of shame? Finally, I had something to grab onto to guide me out of the constant shame spiral of my life.

Over time, this shifted focus in therapy on my newly discovered values of integrity and honesty helped me build a positive self-image. As I learned positive characteristics about myself, I was able to live more in accordance with these values. I wasn't the bad twin who was having to pretend to be the good twin. This had been a myth. I was actually good at my core.

Discovering this—and knowing it deeply—changed everything. Over the course of two years, I was able to slowly let go of shame.

A few years later, I found tangible evidence that I was cured from my shame disorder. My father used to send a batch of his coveted beef jerky every holiday season. I introduced Sarah, now my wife, to it early in our relationship, and soon she joined me in eagerly awaiting the package each year. One Christmas, I was home alone when the package came. My father had sent two one-gallon bags of jerky; one labeled with my name, and one labeled with Sarah's. I saw an opportunity to secretly keep some of the jerky from Sarah. So I decided that I would share my bag with Sarah, but hide hers, keeping the extra supply all for myself. I chose to hide it on a top shelf in the kitchen, placing it inside a little-used pan.

The jerky didn't stay hidden for long. About a week later, my wife had an occasion to reach up there. I was standing in the kitchen, and realized I was about to be caught. She felt the bag before she saw it. As she pulled it down, she looked at me, slowly realizing the jerky betrayal I had committed. I waited for the warm wash of shame to run down my body, for my head to drop, even for tears to come. I knew how much she loved this jerky, and I knew what I had done was wrong in the course of our relationship.

But none of these reactions happened. Instead, I found myself looking back at her and grinning. In that moment, I stood back, amazed at myself. I became aware that I felt no shame for what I had done. At all. None. I was astonished.

Then it hit me: I knew that this deception was not proof that I was an awful person. I was a good person, but I had done something shady. I felt guilty, sure, for trying to pull a fast one on my wife, and I did apologize for the deception. But the anguish of being a horrible person—which I had felt for weeks after taking the oil change coupon—was simply not there. It dawned on me that I had just overcome the shame that had clogged my entire life.

I was so proud of myself, and this pride shone through on my face and body. My wife did not understand my bizarre reaction. Why would I be proud of hiding the jerky? I tried to explain to her the milestone I had just reached. Needless to say, she was not amused. It's okay; she didn't need to be. I knew my shame disorder was cured on that day.

And it turns out that the only way I healed from my depression—and eating disorder, and addiction—was by addressing my shame disorder. I still deal with a fair amount of anxiety, but none of it is connected to feeling shame. Healing my shame was key to all of my recoveries.

Healing 11

The Phenomenal Women's Club

A particular type of client comes into my office on occasion who I've come to dub as members of the "phenomenal women's club." These women are usually in their late 20s or early 30s. Their presenting concerns include anxiety, depression, post-traumatic stress disorder (PTSD), and relationship issues. They have often married early, by the age of 20, and had children. In adulthood, they've usually functioned as overachievers. They report feeling broken, or ill-equipped for life. But I tell them they're actually members of the phenomenal women's club.

I teach them that they're not fundamentally flawed, but instead are having a psychologically normal reaction to their lives. We review their childhood circumstances and experiences, and they almost always disclose years of neglect and abuse, usually from parents who had severe mental illness or substance use disorders. This neglect and abuse produced multiple survival strategies, which therapists call "coping skills." These women almost always have developed a skill in reading the moods of others and sensing how others are feeling. They are very attentive to their children, and are fiercely committed to raising their children in a loving, supportive environment. They've had little guidance in how to do so, but they possess deep, on-target instincts for what good parenting looks like. What they're doing—without knowing it—is breaking the generations of trauma and abuse that were passed down to them.

The experiences of trauma and resultant coping skills have come at a cost. A deep well of shame typically resides within them. They never feel good or worthy. Their history usually includes lower levels of educational achievement than that of their peers, and they mistakenly believe this is because they're not smart. They're full of doubts, having cut themselves off from their internal truth, but they've been trying to gain worth by being perfect. Deep depression, crippling anxiety, or avoidance trauma responses have plagued them for years, and they've usually survived an abusive relationship or two. They come to me desperate for help.

I work with these women to teach them that there's nothing wrong with them; in fact, they are quite phenomenal. I draw lines from their childhood trauma to their current functioning in life. I help them understand that the perfectionism, while crippling in adulthood, was actually very protective in childhood. As a child, they needed to be perfect. They learned they weren't supposed to have needs, and expressing any would just get shame heaped upon them. They knew—often subconsciously—that there was no room for their needs amidst the chaos of the household.

As adults, they usually were overcontrolling. As children, they had so little control or power, so they compensated by trying to dictate and force every-thing in their lives into being when they could. They became very astute at reading a room, because it was always important to know what mood Mom or Dad was in. They learned to be calm in crises; they walked around always expecting the worst to happen. And when it did, there was an eerie sense of calm about them.

Expecting the worst was a very useful skill. If they could anticipate something bad was about to happen, they could try and either head it off or get far away from it.

I work with these phenomenal women to understand all their survival strategies, and more importantly, to thank them for keeping them safe. Once they have done this we begin a process of examining which strategies aren't working anymore, so these can be let go and replaced with healthier methods. These women retain the best parts of their survival strategies—like being able to read a person's moods—but they also learn to temper this with healthy boundaries. They discover that they can read someone's mood, while not feeling responsible for it.

In these ways, we shift their perfectionism into a striving for excellence. They can desire to do their best—in their given circumstances, with their given resources—while also practicing self-compassion whenever they fail or fall short. And they learn that it's okay to have needs; I teach them healthy ways to communicate these to their partners, parents, children, and bosses.

They also learn that the internal shaming dialogue is a voice that has told them stories about themselves and others for years—many of which are false or outdated. We uncover the source of the shame; usually this is a version of *I'm unlovable* or *I'll be abandoned if I mess up*. These beliefs translate into perpetual feelings in their current lives that they will get fired, or divorced. We replace these messages with positive statements, like *no matter what happens, I'm going to be okay,* and *it's okay if this thing that I want doesn't happen.* They come to deeply understand that they are normal, and human, and resilient.

Sometimes this work takes six months; more often than not, it takes a year or two. Watching these women recover is nothing short of amazing. They are some of my favorite clients.

Wounded 7

The Wheels Come Off the Bus

I received my results of the EPPP that November. I had passed. I was going to be a licensed psychologist! This was the pinnacle of twelve years of effort, including one year of graduate school applications, eight years of graduate study, a one-year internship, a one-year fellowship, and one year of supervised practice.

To celebrate, I decided to go on a cruise. Cruises were not a big thing where I came from on the coast of North Carolina, but they were very popular in the upper Midwest. So I chose a small cruise line that catered to gay women and put it on my credit card. The cruise I chose left from Tampa and had stops in Mexico, Belize, and Honduras. It was scheduled for the last week of January into the first week of February.

Throughout the winter, my addiction was raging and was now fully out of control. I had developed tolerance to the sleepy effects of Ambien, so as I've mentioned, I would take them throughout the day for their calming effects. The blackouts did not stop, however, and I regularly blacked out several times a week.

One fateful evening in January, I decided to go shopping for cruising attire at Target. I had a new prescription of Ambien ready, so I picked that up and took several. My memory of the rest of that night is highly grayed out, but here's what I was able to piece together from the police report and the employees at Target.

I spent a couple of hours at Target, and did not want to leave when the store closed at 11. I tried to hide out in the dressing rooms and had a significant altercation with the employees there, wherein I refused to leave. I was rude and accusatory, and I ended up shoplifting a pair of leggings.

Once they finally got me out of Target, I went through a Taco Bell drive-through. I proceeded to drive home. At five minutes past midnight on my 38th birthday, I ran a red light, stopped my car in the middle of the road, and reversed back through the intersection, narrowly missing cars each time. A police officer happened to witness this and pulled me over. I have hardly any memories of this happening. Then I failed a sobriety test, and was arrested for DUI. I was taken to the local police station.

In a search of my car, the officers discovered my bottle of Ambien that I had picked up only hours earlier. Twelve tablets were missing. It's likely that I had taken all twelve over the preceding few hours.

I was fingerprinted and booked. Then I was allowed to call someone to come pick me up. I ran through my sober contacts and tried several NA friends. No one answered. The police were about to lock me up for the night when I finally got through to Johnny at 3 a.m., an NA member with more than 30 years of sobriety. He came and picked me up and got me home.

The next day, I awoke with a very hazy memory of what had happened. I had the paperwork for the arrest, and the location and contact information for the impound lot. I spent my birthday calling in sick to work and taking a cab to the impound lot to retrieve my car. When I got into it, my uneaten Taco Bell meal was still sitting in the passenger's seat. Next, I drove to Target and found one of the employees I had accosted. She explained to me how I had behaved the night before. I profusely apologized to her and paid for the stolen clothes. I felt thoroughly humiliated and ashamed.

Then my addiction kicked in. I needed a cover story. I quickly concocted one and went to my regular Friday night NA meeting, telling everyone that I had driven after taking one Ambien, and that I got a DUI. When I returned to work on Monday, I proactively met with my boss and told her a similar story: that I had a valid prescription for Ambien and had made a bad judgment, taking one while I was out shopping. Since it was so late, I explained that I was trying to go to sleep as soon as possible after getting home. I had thought I had enough time to get home before the effects kicked in.

In most states, licensed health care providers have access to additional resources when they have substance use disorders. Because we're charged with safeguarding the public, we have an ethical obligation to make sure we're healthy enough to serve in our licensed capacities. These agencies work with the provider to structure a recovery plan to support them, and have accountability measures embedded in to track the provider.

In Minnesota, this monitoring program is the Health Professionals Services Program (HPSP). I had heard about it in my time at Hazelden, whenever health care providers came through treatment. I also knew their offices were housed in the same building as my licensing agency. I knew the standard procedure was to self-report any substance use issues to them, which would include this incident. Hazelden also felt obligated to report me to them.

I made the call early one morning. Someone at the agency called me back, and I told them the same false story I peddled to my NA meeting and boss. The case worker on the line expressed doubt that I needed their services, since I had a valid prescription and had not abused it but rather took it at an ill-advised time.

I hung up from this call and exhaled, thinking I was going to get away with everything. A tiny light at the end of the tunnel was starting to enlarge. *I might be able to get out of this scrape*, I thought.

I asked around my recovery community and retained a popular attorney who was also in recovery. I borrowed money from my father (to whom I told the same false story) to pay the DUI fine and lawyer fees. At this point, I thought I was going to be okay.

To a rational, sane person, this would have been enough of a wake-up call to stop using. Not for me. It was still game-on. I was fully out of control at this point.

My cruise was coming up in a few weeks. I learned that most cruises have onshore excursions when they land at each port, offering fun and adventure to their passengers. I had browsed the excursions available at each port and chose things like touring an ancient Mayan site in Mexico, and snorkeling in Honduras. I had also registered for a cave tubing adventure in Belize. Then late one night, a week before the cruise, I suddenly remembered that some friends had bought some prescription drugs in Mexico where they weren't required to have a prescription.

A lightbulb went off in my brain. I then spent hours researching each port I was going to and discovered that Belize has very relaxed control of prescription drugs. In fact, they had two dockside over-the-counter pharmacies that specifically catered to tourists.

Over the next few days I formulated a plan. I withdrew $650 dollars in cash from my bank. I emptied the prescription bottles I had for pills, and then I packed those bottles with the cash in my suitcase.

Once in Tampa, I boarded the cruise and found my room. I was too afraid to try talking to anyone, so I mostly kept to myself. The extent of my involvement with others was asking someone to take my picture at the Mayan ruins we visited in Mexico. My focus was on what was going to happen in Belize.

Once in Belize, I located the two dockside pharmacies I'd researched. I perused them both and took stock of what they had. There were plenty of generic benzodiazepines, generic Ambien, and generic muscle relaxers, but what I was really after was generic opioids. I could only locate one kind, and when I searched the generic name online, it came up as akin to codeine. I was light years beyond the point of being able to get high on codeine. So I was super disappointed.

I went and grabbed lunch to let the news sink in. *Oh well*, I thought, *I might as well make the most of what they've got.* So I returned to the pharmacies and bought hundreds of pills of generic Ambien and various benzos, and threw in some muscle relaxers for good measure. I boarded the ship and pulled out my empty prescription bottles and put the new drugs in there.

I don't remember much of the rest of the cruise. Between the benzos and zolpidem, I was pretty much blacked out for the rest of that week. Then, at our final stop in Honduras, I joined a snorkeling tour. At the conclusion of the tour, we were given a plate of fresh local fruit. I had been extra careful on the ship, so I think this is where I picked up a C. diff infection, which was undiagnosed at this point. Within a couple of days, I was having bouts of diarrhea and cramping. By the time I flew home, I was severely ill. But I don't remember much of this week either, because I continued taking handfuls of pills every day.

Despite my illness, I returned to work as scheduled. By now, my use had progressed to all day, every day, including at work. Every couple of hours, I would walk the halls of Hazelden and duck around the corner or go into a bathroom stall and swallow another few pills. Then I would carry on with the next assessment, the next individual therapy session, the next group.

It was the muscle relaxers that got me caught. About a week after I returned, I was covering the Sunday shift and was the only mental health provider in the building. I had taken too many muscle relaxers, and combined with the dehydration from the bacterial infection, began to lose my normal gait walking down the hall. I stumbled and couldn't walk in a straight line. I was beginning to slur my words.

A staff member called the on-site nursing staff to help me. I don't remember the conversation, because once again, I was in a blackout.

I was told later that I was able to convince them that my balance and speech issues were due to dehydration from the infection, and they allowed me to call a friend who followed my car the six miles home.

I called in sick the next three days. I did finally get to a doctor, and this is where I got my diagnosis of C. diff. Once again, I thought I had enough of a cover story to explain my behavior, and that life would go on as usual.

I was wrong. When I returned to work that Thursday morning, I saw a meeting with the manager of the mental health clinic on my calendar. I walked across the building and entered her office. Sitting across from her desk was the executive director of the facility. *Shit.* This was an intervention.

My boss laid out the evidence before her: a DUI a month ago, followed by the incident on Sunday. She said that she suspected I was using.

I could feel all the color drain from my face. *This is definitely an intervention*, I thought. *At Hazelden, for fuck's sake.*

As she talked, I racked my brain for some thought—some statement that could get me out of this jam. But I knew deep down that I was busted.

At the same time, the shame within me was blocking me. I was too terrified to really reveal how bad off I was. When my boss finished laying out the evidence and asked for my response, the only words I could get myself to say were, "That which you said is not untrue." *That which you said is not untrue.* I couldn't even utter the sentence, "Yes, I've been using. I need help." *That which you said is not untrue.*

I was put on an immediate leave from my position. I ended up going first on short-term, then long-term disability. Because of the law stating that I must be free from chemical use problems for two years—something I'd lied about when I took the job—I knew I was going to lose my position as a mental health professional.

For some reason, this seemed to open my floodgates. *Nothing more to lose now*, I thought. At our next meeting, I confessed my secret life to my NA family in a sobbing mess. I called HPSP and got honest. They recommended I get a substance use assessment and follow their recommendation. I did, and was actually honest with the assessors, telling them every detail of what I had been going through.

I still remember the shocked look on their faces as I revealed the full extent of my secret life. When it came time to make a recommendation, they didn't quite know what to do with me. Here I was, a mental health professional who specialized in treating addiction, and in fact, I was working at arguably the world's most prestigious treatment center. They originally were going to recommend intensive outpatient treatment, where I could remain living at home while receiving care, since I had such an extensive knowledge base, but I knew there was no way I would not use through that. I told them this, and they upgraded their recommendation to a residential program.

In working with my human resources representative at Hazelden, I learned that the three most well-known treatment centers—Hazelden in Minnesota, Betty Ford in California, and Caron in Pennsylvania—had an informal agreement that should any one of their workers need treatment, they would refer them to one of the other two. So I called and arranged an intake with Caron.

I had no money, having spent it all on the cruise and drugs. So I put the plane ticket to Pennsylvania on my credit card, and I arranged for a friend to look after my cats for a month. I packed up two suitcases, and left—completely unsure of what my future held.

It turns out my hell was just getting started.

Healing 12

Newton's Laws of Motion

With the advent of the scientific revolution about 500 years ago, scientists have sought to discover and describe some fundamental laws that seem to exist in the universe, explaining the ways that matter behaves. For example, we have three laws of thermodynamics, one of which states that matter cannot be created or destroyed. We have five laws for gases that describe how they behave. And then we have Newton's three laws of motion, first described in 1686. They state that an object at rest tends to remain at rest, and an object in motion tends to remain in motion; that the acceleration of an object depends on its mass and how much force is applied; and that when one object exerts a force on another object, the second object exerts an equal and opposite force on the first.

I think about Newton's laws a lot when I work with clients. I think they also describe the processes of change in people.

- *An object at rest remains at rest, and an object in motion remains in motion at constant speed and in a straight line unless acted on by an unbalanced force.*

  Here, a rock sitting on the ground will remain still on the ground; it will not spontaneously move unless some force is applied to it. And a ball that's thrown will continue in a straight line, until the force of gravity pulls it down and stops it. It if were in space, a thrown ball would just keep going forever at a constant speed.

People seem to have a similar inertia, in that most people find it easier to keep doing what they're doing, even when it's not productive or helpful. People keep using substances or stay in unhealthy relationships, because it's easier than changing. And people may know they need to get a new job or find a therapist, but they feel inertia pulling them away from initiating this new activity.

When I work from this understanding, I can appreciate just how hard it is to change anything. I often ask clients how long they had my phone number before they made the call to schedule an appointment. They usually say somewhere between six and nine months. I had the number for Peggy for almost a year. In short, change is hard. Changing paths requires the application of mental energy or force, and it means overcoming the inertia of maintaining the status quo.

- *The acceleration of an object depends on the mass of the object and the amount of force applied.*

This law states that for an object to change speed, something must force it to, and how fast it changes speed is related to how much force was applied to it and how massive the object itself is. When a baseball player hits a home run, the speed at which the ball goes out of the park is proportional to how hard the player struck the ball and how heavy the ball is.

I also try to keep this in mind with clients. Once a person has decided to change something about themselves, I appreciate that this takes an enormous outpouring of energy, over and above the regular amount of energy it takes just to exist. And the bigger the change the person is making, the greater the energy they must put into it.

Because of this, therapists often find that helping clients to make smaller, incremental changes over time works better than trying to get clients to make a big change all at once. We know, for example, that if someone wants to start an exercise program, they will find more success if they're asked to engage in successive, small changes—like spending one week just driving to the gym, then the next week going into the gym and staying five minutes, then staying 30 minutes, and so on, until they work up to one hour three times per week. Then they can be asked to start going to the gym for one hour three times a week. Making small changes takes less force/effort—so they tend to happen—versus applying one big outpouring of force/effort to get to a certain place. Most people who try to just jump to the end and go to the gym three times a week for an hour fade away after a few enthusiastic trips.

- *Whenever one object exerts a force on another object, the second object exerts an equal and opposite force on the first.*

Newton's third law of motion says there are consequences for applying force. When a person steps off a boat onto a dock, the boat reacts by moving in the opposite direction. When a rocket takes off, it's because the exhaust from the rocket creates a downward force, which creates an equal and opposite thrust in the upward direction.

This law might be the most important one I use. Because to me, it means that whenever people change, there will be consequences and reactions by other agents in their circles. Because we exist in social systems, there will always be a reaction in the system.

Often this comes in the form of resistance. When a client starts setting healthy boundaries with their families, the families will often react in a way that tries to return the client to their old way of operating. When a person tries to get sober, their using buddies will try to keep them using. Overcoming this opposite reaction is key to long-term adoption of new behaviors.

When I work with a client on making a change, part of the work is to plan for how to deal with this opposite reaction from their social systems. Navigating this last component is ultimately what determines whether the client will be successful.

Healing 13

Get Versus Have

For years, I had heard people in recovery say they were grateful that they never HAD to use again. I never understood them. For me, after eight years of coming to meetings, I fully understood that I would never GET to use again. I knew, in every fiber of my being, that there was no such thing as healthy use for me. I would never be able to use socially. I had abused my right to use so much for so long that I had worked myself into a state where I knew I had ruined that privilege. So for me, it was I never GET to use again. And for the most part I made peace with that.

Years later, several years after my sobriety date had finally stuck, my wife and I were traveling to see her mother. We stopped at a liquor store so she could buy some beer for the cookout they were planning that evening. For some reason, I decided to come into the store and have a look around. Prior to this day, whenever I went into a liquor store, I could only look around and see the walls of forbidden fruit: bottle after bottle of you'll-never-get-to-use-me. I was the fat kid who had to stay behind at the amusement park because I was over the weight limit. I only saw all the ways I was deficient.

But that day, it felt different. As I looked at the towers of bottles and cans, I very clearly connected with a feeling that had been growing in me. After years of therapy, working on myself, and building authentic relationships, I was happy. There was a lightness to my existence. It dawned on me in that moment that I had actually achieved the feeling I was always seeking every time I used. Contented. Peaceful. The wall of alcohol I was looking at held no power over me. It felt amazing. And then I thought about that phrase again, and I finally understood: I never HAD to use again. I never HAD to use to try and get that feeling. I could get it without using. Recovery was giving me that long-sought-after nirvana.

Now, when I hear somebody say they never have to use again, I smile knowingly. Me too. And I understand that my job as a counselor is to help others travel from GET to HAVE.

Wounded 8

Caron

I arrived at the Caron Treatment Center, located in southeastern Pennsylvania, in the evening. I knew that typical protocol was for new arrivals to stay in detox, where their withdrawal from alcohol and drugs could be medically managed. But I hadn't used in five days, meaning I was already through my withdrawal period, so I was admitted straight onto my unit.

What I remember most about this first night was the intake counselor I met with shortly after arrival. His job was to reassess me to make sure I was appropriate for admission, and to orient me to the treatment process. I sat in the chair across from him feeling so ashamed, so broken, so lost. I could hardly make eye contact as I answered his questions. When he learned that I worked at Hazelden, he put down his pen and looked at me with kind eyes.

"You know, I just returned from a relapse six months ago," he said.

I cannot overemphasize the effect that hearing this had on me, that someone who worked at a treatment center could recover, be okay, and return to work at that treatment center. And that he could talk about it. It provided the tiny sliver of hope I needed to believe in the treatment process.

The intake team didn't know quite where to put me. They had general men's and women's units where most first-time admissions went. There, participants would get introduced to the disease model of addiction, and the 12-step solution to it.

They also had a special relapse unit that worked with people who had had previous treatment, achieved some stable sobriety, but then returned to use. There, the patients already knew the fundamentals of 12-step recovery, having lived the principles for usually years. Counselors worked with these patients to identify the string of events that knocked them off their sobriety course and led to a relapse. Sobriety skills were sharpened, and a solid relapse prevention plan was identified.

I didn't fit neatly into either of these groups. This was my first time getting sober and going to treatment, but I had eight years of active engagement in 12-step programs and worked at a facility that was based on these principles. I knew the steps, I knew the traditions, I knew the slogans. Hell, I taught them to patients every day. I had spent years trying everything the program said I needed to do to be sober. I had tried everything, that is, except stopping my use. I'd gone to three to four meetings a week, sometimes serving as chair. I'd worked with a sponsor. I'd shared at meetings about personal issues I was struggling with. I'd completed a fourth-step inventory and read it aloud to my sponsor. I'd worked on my underlying issues to become a better person. I'd taken a daily inventory. I don't know if I thought that if I worked the program hard enough, my desire to use would leave me, but I'd approached it like this was the case. But of course, my desire never left. I just kept digging the hole deeper until I could no longer see the sky above.

In the end, the intake team decided to put me on the relapse unit, while also using some of the treatment materials from the general units. They thought I would blend in better with the relapse patients than with first-timers, and much of residential treatment relies on peer interaction.

Days earlier when I had called my family to let them know I was an addict—and that I had lost my job and needed to go to treatment—I only asked for one thing: that each of them attend the Caron family program the third week of my treatment. They all were flabbergasted at learning of my secret life, but they agreed.

I settled into treatment and set about on a determined path of sobriety. I completed all the treatment assignments to the best of my ability. I shared honestly in my group—giving my full addiction timeline over the course of two hours one day. It was the first time I had let anyone see all of me. I shared about how once I drank three-day-old water from my cat's bowl, because I discovered that I had dropped some pills in it that were partially dissolved. I cried. I read the NA basic text. I met with my counselor and discussed my progress. At this point, I can say I genuinely wanted to be sober.

This feeling wouldn't last.

As suspected, I did blend in well with the relapse unit patients. After they got over the disbelief that someone like me, working where I worked, could have hidden her addiction so well, they took me in as one of them.

When my mother, father, and two sisters came for the family program, my treatment team put us all in the first-timers track, since this was the first time my family was learning of my addiction. They came in from all over: North Carolina, Atlanta, Washington, DC, and even Alaska to be there.

In the first-timers' track, they attended psychoeducational groups, outlining how addiction hijacks the brain and how to best help their loved one recover. In the center of the room was always a stuffed animal, meant to symbolize addiction. The goal for most of these meetings was to personify the addiction as separate from their loved ones. To develop love and understanding for the family member, and to see the addiction as something that was happening to them too.

In several of the groups, the patient would join the family, and complete activities designed to help their relationships. Eventually, it was time for our family to be a part of this group—together with three other families. It was only the second time we had all been in the same room together since my parents' divorce 18 years earlier. We had pretty much split up and lived separate lives in separate states, only coming together occasionally in 2s or 3s. The other time we were all together was for my doctoral graduation. *I guess I have a way of bringing my family together*, I thought wryly as we sat down.

One of our group activities used art therapy and had a profound impact on me. Family members were given a large piece of paper and instructed to draw what it was like to live with their addict's addiction. They were then invited to share their artwork with the rest of the group and talk about their feelings. The purpose of the activity is to communicate to the person with the substance use disorder how their addiction has impacted people in their life. Most of the time, the addict can only see the hurt and pain they feel, and have a hard time seeing how their addiction has caused distress in others. The exercise usually elicits strong emotions and lots of tears.

In our group, family member after family member showed pictures illustrating rage, sadness, hurt, fear, and despair. Sometimes, after hearing what their addiction had done to their parents, spouse, or children, the patient would go to them in tears and apologize. This allowed for an emotional reunion of the addict back into the family.

Then it was time for my family to share. Both my mother and father turned over completely blank pages. They had drawn nothing on them. My mother talked about having no idea I was using, and therefore having lived with no reaction or feelings about it. My father shared much the same sentiment.

I had this weird feeling inside me. I was glad that I had shielded them from the worst effects of my addiction, but it was also clear that I didn't have much of a relationship with either one of them. This had been by design. I knew my addiction affected me, but I purposefully withdrew from relationships with family and others to keep my addiction from destroying anyone else's life. I had just spent three years meeting with families devastated by their loved ones' addictions, and I intentionally structured my life not to produce the same result. This had seemed to work for my parents.

The same could not be said for my sisters. My older sister's picture really stood out to me. In it, she had drawn a black, simple stick figure in each of the corners, and a whorl of colored lines in the center. As she shared her picture, she said that each of the four stick figures represented herself, our younger sister, our father, and mother, and that the tangle of colored lines in the center represented me. She described our family as being generally separated, but connected by the "big ball of chaos" that was me.

This hit something deep inside of me. *She doesn't even see me as a person*, I realized. Devastated, I became tearful.

I looked at her and said with hurt, "I don't even get to have a body in your picture."

Years later, I would come to understand her point of view. In most dysfunctional families, one person becomes the "identified patient." This person gets all the focus; they are always the one in trouble or not functioning well. Much time and attention is given to this person. This myth, while holding some truth, serves to maintain the dysfunction in the family, as no one has to look at themselves. However, in dysfunctional families, every member has issues.

This was how my sister had experienced our family. I was the one with the known mental health problems in childhood. I was the one with the eating disorder that was sent to treatment in college. And now I was the one whom everyone had to come together for, to support her recovery. Something deep inside of me reacted to that—to being labeled as the thing that was wrong with our family. I was just a tangled scribble of lines to her—total chaos.

Part of the family program also included an individual family therapy session with the patient. My counselor and the director of the health care professionals program attended to facilitate. When it was over, my family left, and I stayed to process the session with the two counselors. I thought it had gone rather well. We had shared honestly with each other.

Immediately when the door closed, the counselors looked at each other knowingly and deeply exhaled, shaking their heads.

"Oh my," one counselor shared. "Your family is one of the most shaming families we've ever worked with."

I was shocked. I had absolutely no awareness of this.

They then pointed out statement after statement that labeled me as a bad person. At one point, one family member had shaken their finger at me and said in anger, "My god, you, of all people, should know better!"

This was the beginning of my shame awareness.

Weeks later, once I had returned home, I received a card from my sister.

On the front was an abstract drawing of a circle. The front of the card said, "There is a circle of caring all around . . .," and the inside said, ". . . and you are right in the middle." My sister had drawn in a stick figure body in the circle. Inside she wrote, "You have a body. Use it wisely." Going through this exercise fundamentally changed our relationship with each other.

In an ironic twist, I found out I had been granted licensure as a psychologist on my final day in treatment. Before I came to Caron, I was working with individuals with substance use disorders and helping them recover while secretly succumbing to my own addiction. Now, I was openly receiving treatment for my addiction, and the state had just recognized me as an official psychologist, giving me freedom to work with people, but because of the 2-year law, I was no longer allowed to work with them directly.

As part of my licensure, I was stipulated to enroll in the state's monitoring program for licensed health care professionals, which I did. I was assigned a case worker. I agreed to meet with a therapist weekly, and to have quarterly reports on my progress sent to the agency from my therapist, psychiatrist, boss, and sponsor. I also agreed to random drug tests.

For the drug test, I was assigned two colors. I would have to call a phone number each morning, and if either one of my colors was called, I would need to submit a urine drug test before the end of the day.

As I heard all of this, I pictured myself succeeding. I truly thought I would.

But my sincere desire to get sober didn't last.

I was released from treatment after 31 days, with a recommendation to step down to an intensive outpatient treatment program in my home area. I made it as far as the airport. When I boarded the flight to take me home, I called the pharmacy to refill my last standing prescription for Ambien. I was falling prey to a common addict trope: I just wanted to use One. More. Time. *I didn't get to say goodbye to my drugs, you see, and if I could just use one more time, I could have complete closure and be ready to live the rest of my life sober.* Addiction really is a cunning disease.

However, when I called the pharmacy, there was a problem.

"This refill has expired," the pharmacy tech said as the engines revved for takeoff. "It looks like it hasn't been filled in more than six months. If you can get your doctor to resubmit a prescription, we'd be happy to fill it."

That really should have been the end of it. It wasn't.

My *one-more-time* idea was firmly planted. *I need to somehow get ahold of Vicodin again to say goodbye,* I told myself. *Opioids really were my preferred drug, so it's okay that I was denied the refill of Ambien.*

The plane landed, and I was joyfully picked up by two close friends in recovery. I returned home and enrolled in an intensive outpatient program (IOP) that specialized in working with women with trauma histories. We met four days a week, three hours at a time. I started to get to know the other women in the group. Here, too, we had to submit to random drug screens.

However, my desire to use one-more-time grew until it was untenable.

Healing 14

Higher Power

My biggest obstacle to 12-step recovery—indeed, most people's biggest obstacle—was its focus on spirituality. The second step dictates that we develop a belief in a "power greater than ourselves," and the third step asks us to "turn our will and our life over" to this power. The word *God* is used to describe this in the remaining steps.

If there was one thing I felt I knew for sure, it was that there was no God. I had never believed. My family was not a religious one. Prayer was not a part of our family life, nor was passing on stories from the Bible. But as Southern culture dictated, we were members of a local church and attended the weekly Sunday service.

One of my earliest memories—I think I was about four—was sitting in a pew in church, listening to the pastor, and thinking, *I just don't get it.* This talk about a man in the sky who knew everything I did or thought made no sense to me. But everyone around me seemed to think this, so I kept my thoughts secret.

When I was an adolescent, I was part of the church's youth group. This was what the adolescents in my town did. We did service projects, had Bible study, and participated in lock-ins, but all the while, I maintained my secret belief—or lack thereof. The *God belief* in others seemed so strong, I thought maybe something was wrong with *my* mind. My grandmother was extremely religious, attending church several times a week, and devoting her life to God. I knew my life would be easier if I believed like everyone else did, but it really did seem beyond my capacity.

I finally made peace with it early in high school when I decided that if there was a God and I ended up before him, he would think more highly of me for being true to myself and my beliefs than if I simply tried to believe things other people told me. For some reason, that thought brought me some peace. I let go of trying to believe.

So I lived my life without God. And I knew to keep this a secret; it would have meant immediate rejection from my community to voice my belief.

I made adjustments that worked for me. When we recited the pledge of allegiance in school, I left out the words "in God." When our family attended church, I always volunteered to staff the nursery downstairs, which would excuse me from participating in worship. I did go through confirmation and was baptized along with my peers, but I did this purely for social survival. I had zero personal convictions.

As I've outlined earlier, I was 17 when I was first introduced to 12-step recovery. I showed up for treatment hopeful. On my second day there, I was introduced to the 12 steps of Overeaters Anonymous. But the second I heard the word *God*, it was over. All of my hope immediately drained out of me.

I participated in OA meetings while I was in treatment, but I experienced them exactly as I had church: as something to go along with to avoid rejection of the group, while never internalizing. I went on with my life into my 20s.

So when my counselor Peggy first suggested I attend an Overeater's Anonymous group again at age 28, I patiently explained to her my history with God, and that it was just not possible for me to get help there. She listened, shared she still felt it could help me, but didn't push it. And so our dance around this began.

Usually once every few sessions, she would gently revisit the topic. At first I thought she just didn't understand how deep my disbelief was in God, so I would embark on a more detailed history. She persisted, and then I started to be annoyed. *Clearly she is not hearing what I was telling her. Why did she keep bringing it up?*

For a year and a half, we battled over this. She gently held firm that it could be helpful; I dismissed every suggestion to try it. At some point, I felt she finally understood my intense aversion to God. She was still suggesting I go, so finally, I gave in and made a plan to go. It really was a testament to the amount of trust I had in her.

Turns out she was right. These were definitely my people. But the God thing still bothered me. I felt I had found something helpful, but I still had a deep aversion to the God language. For the first six years I attended 12-step meetings, I would not even say the word God. I either declined to do the reading, or substituted the term Higher Power. I participated in the parts of the program that had nothing to do with God.

After being in the program for about three years, I understood that in order to recover, some kind of belief had to be developed. Some members would derisively suggest that I make the doorknob my Higher Power—that it didn't matter, as long as my Higher Power wasn't me. I found this remark to be dismissive and judgmental. I knew this wouldn't work for me. So I did what I always did: set about a dedicated goal to study, explore, and learn. I was going to conquer this problem academically.

As an aside, I was always interested in Christian history. As a classics major in undergrad, I had taken a course on the birth of Christianity. I was fascinated with how this set of beliefs had developed and taken over most of the world. So I had a little background in religious studies. I also owned a few books in comparative religious studies. I thought, *Surely, there's a system of thought out there that can work for me.* And so I read. Judaism and Islam were out, as they were based on the same Abrahamic God as Christianity. I was drawn to many of the concepts of eastern religions, especially Buddhism, with its focus on overcoming suffering, of which I'd had lots of experience. While I found various parts of many different religions interesting, none resonated internally. I couldn't find a system of beliefs that explained the world and the people in it to me.

One of the final years of my doctoral study included a required class, basically on the history of science. It was a survey course meant to situate psychology in the wider field of scientific study. We read a number of books on the history of science in the course, but one completely hooked me. It was about the study of complexity theory at the Santa Fe Institute in the 1980s. The more I learned about this thing called complexity theory, the more excited I got. Here was something I completely resonated with. Slowly, over time, I realized, *Science is how I organize and understand the world and the people in it. Science is my religion.*

And so I set off to understand complexity theory. The Santa Fe Institute gathered a group of economists and physicists to each bring their varied expertise to the matter. It was known that many systems develop complexity, meaning that an overarching order develops in a system without an overarching hand guiding it. A large number of seemingly independent agents, responding only to nearby conditions, can assemble themselves into an organized whole.

Our world is full of these complex systems. A flock of birds develops complexity, for example; it is full of individual members responding only to their immediate neighbors, but the system as a whole becomes organized into a flock. Our immune system is a complex system, and so are local and global economies (this is why it made sense to put a group of economists and physicists together to study this).

The researchers at the Santa Fe Institute wanted to figure out what conditions let complexity arise. They were able to learn that when a system is completely locked, with no moving agents, or when a system has complete chaos, with only random movements, complexity isn't possible. But they identified a thin line where these two types of systems meet, and that's where something amazing happens. When a system has a bit of structure, but also is loose enough to allow some movement and change, a spontaneous order develops.

They think this is how life formed. All life represents a complex system. Chemical compounds present in the early Earth—which had some structure—through random meetings with other chemical compounds, by chance developed an autocatalytic system. That is, they created a structure that could replicate itself. Over billions of years, these simple proteins evolved into more complex amino acids, which evolved into more complex single-celled organisms, which evolved into more complex multiple-celled organisms. And so on, to the creation of humans.

This provided an explanation of life that did not include a creator God. I resonated deeply with this, and realized this was the system of thought that I utilized to make sense of the world. But back to how it connects with finding a Higher Power. Paradoxically, complexity theory says there is no Higher Power. But Step Two dictates I must find something to turn my life over to. So I decided to turn my life over to complexity theory. I reasoned that I operated at my best when I lived in the conditions that produced complexity. By that, I mean I needed a certain amount of structure in my life, but I also had to hold open space for change and opportunity to come in. My life needed to be organized to some degree, but also needed flexibility to respond to new things in new ways. This abstract focus on the balance between structure and openness was what I defined as my Higher Power.

It was great that I had found a system of beliefs that worked for me, but it wasn't enough. I thought if I could figure out my religious beliefs, sobriety would follow. But this did not happen for me. I had thought that finding a system of beliefs was what was fundamental to developing one's spirituality. But spirituality is more than just how one makes sense of our existence; it is also about feeling deeply connected to things around us. This was what was missing from my previous attempt. I had definitely found a system of beliefs that explained the world to me, but it did not include any component of connection.

I now know that understanding how the world works is not the same as opening yourself up for help, which really is the essence of Step Two. And so my addiction continued for another eight years.

When I made my next sincere attempt at recovery, I was once again faced with the challenge of Step Two. I realized my first run at the step had been almost entirely an academic exercise. It's no wonder it didn't yield sobriety. But this time, my desperation was higher.

This time, I decided that I would visualize my Higher Power as the supportive people in my life—those who I knew loved me and wanted good things for me. This included a number of people in the program I had come to know quite well, along with some close friends and family. Whenever I was faced with a choice, I would visualize all these people standing in a circle around me. I would feel warm love coming from them. I would imagine what they wanted for me, and then try to make decisions that moved me toward this outcome. When faced with a choice, to be honest about something, say, or how to spend my time, I would think, *What would they want for me?* The answer was always that they would want me to take care of myself, they would want me to be a good person, they would want me to do the right thing. I used this to guide my behavior.

In this way, I was finally able to work steps two and three. I finally believed in something outside of myself that could help me, and I made the conscious decision to rely on this imagined group for guidance. My definition of a Higher Power explicitly denied any religious explanation of the world, but it finally did what the steps said needed to happen: we must find and feel a sense of connection to something outside of ourselves, and we must prioritize this connection over our own thoughts and decisions about what should happen.

It turns out that I didn't really need to figure out my religious beliefs in order to work these steps at all. I didn't need to have a system of thought or belief that explained how the world worked. I certainly didn't need to develop a belief in God. The funniest thing is that it was only *after* working steps two and three that was I able to develop spiritual beliefs, this deep feeling of love and connection to others.

I became aware of this about three years into my sobriety. I was talking with a student who was going through a personal crisis. I was offering support, and I shared some of the difficulties I'd had getting through graduate school. At some point in this conversation, I became aware that the student was looking at me exactly the same way I'd looked at my mentors when I was in school, with admiration and veneration. I was amused at first; if she only knew what a mess I had been! Then suddenly, I could see how it was all connected. I felt this wide, powerful river of healing wisdom swirling around me that had been passed down through generations of women—to my mentors, helping them heal, then to me, helping me heal—and now I was passing it down to help someone else heal. I felt deeply connected to generations of women who had made a way out of no way. I felt this energy surrounding me, and I felt connected to all of life—deep within me, in every cell of my being.

I suddenly realized I was having a spiritual experience. Finally, after 14 years in the program! It was a very long journey.

When I had this realization, I thought about something discussed in the Big Book. It includes many mentions of the need to have a "spiritual experience," and that this is the only path to recovery. An appendix at the end of the book offers some comment as to what comprises a "spiritual experience." Here, the authors describe it as a "personality change" that brings about recovery.

That day, I thought about how my personality had completely changed—from being fear- and shame-based to being open, accepting, loving and curious. My personality had indeed changed; ergo, according to this passage, I must have had AA's "spiritual experience" somewhere along the way! There had been no blinding light, no appearance of Jesus. Just this deep feeling of connection, of love, for myself, and for and from others.

Only later was I able to situate this spiritual experience into my scientific system of beliefs. I now believe that as humans, we evolved to connect to others. We have a biological drive to attach to others. This drive was developed because it conveyed better survival odds to early humans. And experiencing connection produces good feelings in our brains and bodies, so that we remain motivated to stay connected even when things get difficult.

Further, an integral feature of being human is our ability to make meaning. We evolved to condense information down into meaningful packets, and then to act on them.

I now believe that as humans, because of our innate drives to connect and make meaning, we all need some system of spirituality. I believe some people have come to interpret the good-connection feelings our bodies and brains produce as religion. Many people create distinct beliefs to explain the powerful biological feelings they get when they connect, and I now know whatever form that belief takes for someone is fine. For many people, the idea of a God works in this capacity—to connect them to something that feels all-good. This makes sense of their experience of the world.

For years, I had been told the only path to recovery was one with a God. I've now come to understand it differently. To explain it, I make a comparison to our nutritional needs. We all need sources of protein for survival. For years, I was told the only source of protein was animal meat. But all the while, I was a spiritual vegetarian. Meat wasn't an option for me, so I made do in a meat-eating world—avoiding meat while suffering spiritual malnutrition. I've come to understand that everybody needs protein, but not everybody needs meat. For me, I've had to identify alternative plant-based sources of protein, of which there are many. Turns out, tons of people are spiritual vegetarians.

My journey to a Higher Power was longer and more difficult than it needed to be. I do believe that the staunch traditionalist view that the 12 steps should never be altered keeps a lot of people from recovery. I have found that many people who do believe in God have a hard time understanding how excluding it is to constantly refer to a Higher Power as "God," as it does in the 12 steps, and in all the 12-step literature. There is even a chapter in the Big Book called

"We Agnostics," which I found highly offensive. It basically says that people who don't believe in God are in denial, and just need to accept the fact that there is a creator God. This system of beliefs excluded me from recovery for over a decade.

Now, when I'm working with people who are trying a 12-step approach to life, I encounter many who stop, as I did, at the mention of God. I sometimes share my story and journey with the program's focus on spirituality. In the beginning, I encourage them to focus on the essence of the step, which is to stop trying to control every single thing in life, to open up to others and rely on guidance from those further along the path of healing. I no longer emphasize a need to develop a system of beliefs that explains how the world works. Now I know this only develops later, as a consequence of going through this process. I help them understand the difference between protein and meat, and figure out what a healthy spiritual diet is for them.

Wounded 9

Nadir

After I returned home from Caron, I attended an outpatient group four days a week. I returned to my regular 12-step meetings and added in several more. My treatment team had not cleared me to return to work, so I had a lot of free time. I met regularly with a new sponsor and diligently worked the steps.

I did not talk about my attempt to get my last prescription of Ambien in any of these meetings. I did not talk about my desire to use *one. last. time.* I knew I should. I knew what happened to people who didn't.

I was sitting at home one Saturday night, the desire to use growing desperate, when I hatched what I knew was a ridiculous plan. I decided I would go out to a club downtown and randomly approach people to ask if they had any drugs.

I got dressed and headed out just after midnight. I decided to go to a gay club, as I felt my chances were highest there. Inside, I walked up to a few men.

"I'm looking for some drugs," I shouted over the music. "Do you have any?" Most could hardly understand what I was saying, and those who could looked at me like I was crazy and simply said no or walked away.

I moved my operation outside. It was close to closing time, so I thought

I could catch people as they were leaving. One young woman was leaning against a wall smoking a cigarette.

"I'm looking to party," I told her directly.

She looked at me for a few seconds before responding. "I'm going to an afterparty. You can follow me if you want."

I hurried back to my car and got behind her as she pulled out of the parking lot. *Jackpot.* We drove about 15 minutes to a suburb and pulled up to a modest house. I followed her inside and was introduced to four of her friends, all guys. They were passing around a meth pipe.

I had never done meth. I was familiar with it, sure. Most of the guys in my Friday night NA meeting were recovering meth addicts. Many of the people I had counseled in treatment used meth. But I had never really had any desire to do meth.

That night, it looked like meth was the only thing available. So I asked them to instruct me on how to use it. One of them held the lighter under the bulb of the pipe, and I could see smoke emitting from the rock. I put my mouth around the tube and inhaled. Then I sat down and waited for the effects to hit me. I knew I was supposed to feel euphoria, powerful, and confident. I felt nothing. The rest of the group settled down into their highs.

I used a couple of more times that night, but still felt nothing. I asked if anyone had opioids, but this was definitely not an opioid crowd. One of the guys there was a marijuana dealer. I got his number, so I could contact him later to see if he could get me any opioids. Then I went home around sunrise, disappointed.

I started texting with the marijuana dealer, and he invited me over to his apartment on several occasions. I would go some nights after my IOP group. He seemed intrigued that I was an addiction psychologist. I smoked marijuana with him a couple of times, but really, I was just working him for opioids. He never came through.

I'd also gotten the number of the meth dealer at the party, so I reached out to him. He didn't have a car and asked if I could drive him around for "a few errands." I did. Several times. Sometimes a couple of his associates would join him.

I never asked what any of the errands were for. They were always late at night, usually after 11 p.m. One time, I was driving three of them.

"Stop at this gas station," one of them instructed. We were in a very sketchy area of town. I pulled into the parking lot and found a spot. Then a police officer pulled into the spot beside me. I felt my stomach drop and prayed that he didn't come over to my car. *How in the world can I explain my being there?* I wondered.

Another time, they asked me to drive them to a casino outside of town.

"Hey, remember you can't bring your gun in," one of them said to the other as we arrived. He left it in my car. I waited for 30 minutes for them to come out again.

"Can you help me get Vicodin?" I asked them often. The meth dealer was able to call around, and one day he found the mother of a friend who had a few Vicodin left over from a surgery. We drove north and pulled up to a ranch house with a nice yard. The meth dealer went in and came out a few minutes later with eight pills. I frantically swallowed them all at once. Even the meth dealer looked at me with concern.

In the space of three months, I had gone from being a respected mental health practitioner at the nation's most prestigious treatment center to a desperate junkie, reduced to providing dealers with late night rides to dangerous places. At this point, I was randomly drug tested at my treatment center, but I tampered with my test one week by taking part of someone else's urine sample and using it as mine.

Outside of treatment, I had little structured time. I would usually attend a 12-step meeting once a day, and I had therapy once a week. For someone who was used to working 50-plus hours a week, I was left with a lot of time on my own. I was also carrying the grief and shame of losing my job.

I had achieved my goal. I had used opioids *one. last. time.* But instead of shutting the door, it opened more widely. Almost immediately, the craving for more came.

Over the next few days, it became clear I was not going to stop using. As I sat with this realization, I came to understand that maybe addiction had gotten to me so early that every fiber of my being was always going to be an addict. *If it's true I was already an addict by the time I was five, maybe my brain was hard wired from childhood and will never change,* I reasoned.

As I had this realization, I knew there was only one outcome for me: I would have to commit suicide. *It's the kindest thing I can do for myself and everyone around me,* I told myself. If the rest of my life was going to be spent going from one addiction to another, living a miserable life, this was the best outcome I could hope for. A feeling of great calm came over me as my perspective on this sharpened. This felt like the most rational, logical thought I'd ever had. I became focused and started planning.

It took almost three weeks to carry out the plan. One of my friends who was in Al-Anon recovery, Richard, had been battling cancer for years. He had just had another surgery. I had never been particularly close to him, but guessed that he probably had a supply of drugs I could use.

I contacted him and offered to come see him—to keep him company as he recovered and do some light housework and cooking for him, I told him. I spent a few days with him. We watched movies in his basement and talked. And over the course of a few visits, I discovered where his prescriptions were kept. I stole just enough so he wouldn't notice. Vicodin—check. Ambien—check.

I decided to carry out my plan on a Monday in May. I skipped my outpatient treatment that I was supposed to go to. I did this by design; I figured this was the easiest way to get someone to check on me. Usually, when a patient no-call-no-shows, their counselor reaches out to them the following day. This way, I thought, my body wouldn't have decomposed very much. Otherwise, it could be weeks before someone came to look for me.

At about six in the evening, I sat down on my couch. I had in front of me five Vicodin, five Ambien, three Trazadone, and nine Benadryl—all picked because they were sedating.

I took all 22 pills, washing them down with a soda.

I then moved to my bedroom. I laid down on the bed. I'd brought a plastic trash bag with me, which I now put over my head. Then I sealed it around my neck with masking tape. My plan was to have the pills knock me out, leaving me to suffocate in the bag. I felt calm and at peace the whole time.

I had left a folded note taped to my apartment door. It read:

> *I'm so sorry for all*
> *the damage I'm leaving. If*
> *I could clean it up I would.*
> *I tried, but my life is too*

painful. I'm truly truly sorry

for causing this pain.

I included my estimated time of death, to help out the medical examiner. In a weird twist, the ink in my pen ran out toward the end of the note, making the last three lines only faintly legible. I remember thinking, *I can't even write a suicide note without messing up.*

Within a few minutes, moisture started collecting around the bottom of the bag from my exhalations. My breathing changed, and I began to hyperventilate, but I remained conscious. I remember observing my body as it hyperventilated; I knew this was an adaptive response. The reflexive deep and rapid breathing was my body trying to decrease the carbon dioxide that was building up in my blood.

I carried on this way for about 45 minutes. My body felt nowhere near the point of passing out from the drugs, and the hyperventilation was causing a massive headache. *Why am I not passing out?* I asked myself. *I should have by now.*

Finally, defeated, I removed the bag from my head. I went back to my living room and gathered all the prescription medications I had in the apartment. I counted them out: 9 Buspar, 32 Welbutrin, 11 Lexapro, 50 Mirapex, 20 acetaminophen, and 18 ibuprofen.

I took all 140 pills, a mixture of antidepressants, anti-anxiety meds, restless leg syndrome medications, and over the counter acetaminophen and ibuprofen. After a bit, my body started to jerk, and I was unable to walk. The room started to spin. I remember falling in the hallway on my way back to the bedroom and vomiting. Then I passed out.

I woke up a few hours later. I was still alive. *Shit.*

Healing 15

Suicide

Screening and assessing for suicide risk is a critical skill for every counselor. Every counseling student is taught the basics of this process in their training program:

1. First, ask direct questions regarding any suicide thoughts. *Have you ever had thoughts of suicide? Have you ever wished you could die? Are you having those thoughts now?*

2. If the patient indicates the presence or history of thoughts, get more details regarding the content, frequency, and distress of the thoughts, using open-ended questions. *Tell me about your thoughts. How often do you have them? What do they consist of?*

3. Once that has been thoroughly explored, move into screening for suicidal behavioral. *Have you ever done anything to hurt yourself? Have you ever taken steps to die?*

4. Assess the client for any identified methods or timelines, and find out if they have established any current plan for suicide. If there's been more than one incident, get details for the worst one and most recent one. *What did you do? What happened as a result? Do you have any plans right now?*

5. Assess for any protective factors that stop the client from carrying out any plan. *Is there anything in your life that you want to live for? What kinds of support do you have when you feel bad?*

6. Then the counselor determines the severity of current risk. If the risk is low, counselors talk to the client about what to do if the thoughts get worse. If the risk is higher, we are mandated by state laws to take steps to remove the possibility of the client carrying out a plan.

Suicide is discussed as if it is a single construct, and suicidal patients are conceptualized to exist along a single continuum, from no thoughts to thoughts to plan to intent to attempt to completion. I've come to understand that there seem to be fundamentally two different types of suicidal patients.

To be honest, dealing with a suicidal patient used to scare the shit out of me. When I was a new clinician, any time I had to work with a client around their suicidal thoughts and behaviors, I felt great apprehension. I worried that I would do something wrong. I felt a responsibility that was beyond my skill. Our training places a heavy emphasis on the importance of helping clients with suicidal thoughts and behaviors, and I just felt inept. The stakes seemed really high, and I felt intense pressure to get it right.

Part of this was because of my own history with suicide. I had suicide attempts in my personal history, and frequent suicidal thoughts were part of my everyday life. How in the world could I be equipped to help someone else with their thoughts, when I hadn't figured out how to handle my own?

One day, a mentor completely changed my feelings and intimidation around suicide. She explained that, at its heart, thoughts of suicide are just a person having an *intense* desire for things to be different in their life. I sat with that definition for a minute. Suddenly, the special place I had relegated suicide to dissolved, and I was no longer afraid of it. I could sit with a person who had an intense desire for things to be different. I knew a lot about that.

This new definition also helped me understand myself better. For years, I had wondered why my mind so often wandered to thoughts of suicide. I knew something was wrong with me, but I didn't understand it. This new perspective allowed me to see how thinking about suicide had actually been helpful—easing my current pain. When my emotional pain got too intense, my mind wandered to scenarios where I could be dead and therefore not have to feel any pain again. In those times, I was not capable of soothing myself by imagining a situation where my life could be improved, so my mind came up with a solution by fantasizing about a time and place where the pain wouldn't exist anymore. In short, it created a situation where my life would be different. Although these thoughts were unpleasant, they were less painful than the deep depression and anxiety I was dealing with. Suicidal thinking was soothing. It was saving me from feeling very painful emotions.

For me, the lifting of suicidal thoughts was one of the biggest milestones of my recovery. It happened gradually. One day when I was having to face a difficult situation, I became aware that I wished I could be really sick instead. I didn't want to die, but I still didn't want to have to go through the experience. I recognized this as an improvement in my mental health. Instead of fantasizing about death, my mind would picture myself in some hospital bed, being taken care of by a medical team. Even though it was still an unhealthy way to cope, I saw it marked a level of healing. *I'm getting better*, I said to myself, smiling as I had this realization.

Now, when I work with clients around suicide, I work to situate myself in relation to their pain. I ask all the required questions, but I also seek to answer the question: *what is it that this person is wishing could be different?* I conceptualize the suicidal thoughts as the best tools their minds have created for soothing their internal pain. I work to see the pain that the person is struggling with, to bear witness to that pain, to let the client see that I am not afraid of that pain. Then I work to instill hope in the patient that there are better ways to soothe their pain.

For clients at low risk, I help them to understand the function of their suicidal thoughts. Instead of trying to get the patient to not have those thoughts, I help them understand that these thoughts are their minds signaling to them that it is overwhelmed and unable to cope with the current situation. I monitor these thoughts as indicators of how much distress the client is in; if a client experiences a sudden increase of thoughts, I know we need to slow down the pace of treatment and help the client utilize some basic coping skills.

In this way, we use the client's suicidal thoughts together to measure how well the treatment is working—instead of treating them as some dreadful thing that I, as a clinician, must deal with. In this process, suicidal thoughts can be honored and listened to.

But when people reach the same point I encountered after I returned from Caron, something different is going on. Those thoughts of suicide weren't just my mind lessening its pain by fantasizing about death; I had clear, goal-directed behavior with the intention of ending my life. My determination was fueled by a complete lack of hope. Looking back, I'm still so struck at how calm and resolute and centered I felt. This was not my mind coping with emotional pain; this was my mind solving a logical problem.

I now understand that these types of suicidal thoughts and behaviors represent a fundamental shift in a person. This is not coping; this is a crisis, and should be treated differently by the mental health providers. The person is no longer strangely comforted by these thoughts. Instead, the person has entered a sort of *delusional* state and is no longer thinking rationally—even if it feels rational to them, as it did to me. It amazes me what the human mind can do. When a person has entered this area, immediate steps must be taken to protect the patient's life, by removing their ability to act on their desires.

Thinking about these fundamental differences in a person experiencing suicidal thoughts and behaviors helps guide me in how to respond.

Healing 16

Pain + Acceptance

There is a well-known concept in Buddhism: in life, pain is inevitable, but suffering is optional. The Four Noble Truths—considered the foundation of Buddhism—outline that this suffering and dissatisfaction is called *dukkha*.

I often find myself working with clients on this concept. I show them two equations:

1. Pain + Acceptance = Pain
2. Pain + Nonacceptance = Suffering

Buddhist philosophy states that we struggle not with the fact that bad things happen, but with our attachment to a non-reality outcome.

Enlightenment is the path of healing, leading us to radical acceptance of every moment, situation, and person. I use this to define acceptance for my students and patients as "letting go of *every* desire that this person, situation, or thing be any different than *exactly* as it is." It forms the basis of my see-accept-join philosophy of counseling, described earlier.

I personally experience this phenomenon every fall. I live in Minnesota, which has very harsh winters. I live here not only because of my job, but because my wife has lived here for her entire life, and she wants to be close to her family here. Every fall, as the sunset slides from 9:00 p.m. down to 4:30 p.m., I experience an anguish.

Ugh, I whine every day, Now the sunset is down to 5:30....It's getting too cold.... Yuck.... Why does it have to snow so soon....?.....I hate this....Fuck, that wind kills....Why do we live here...?

In short, I'm living in a place of nonacceptance and subsequently suffering terribly. This goes on for about six weeks.

Then, one day, I have a conversation with myself where I say, *You knew Minnesota had cold winters; what were you expecting would happen this fall? Why are you wishing for 60 degrees, when clearly this is an impossibility? Why can't you let go of your wish for things to be different?* Over the course of about a week, I'm able to slip back into a place of acceptance. I let go of my desire for the situation to be different and move forward in the present with acceptance of the actual reality.

Winters in Minnesota *are* cold and dark. This is the reality. I'm still cold, to be sure, but I'm no longer suffering. I reach a place of acceptance.

Twelve-step recovery also has many themes around acceptance. Each of the 12 steps has a specific principle attached to it, like Willingness, or Humility, and the principle behind Step One is acceptance. Step One calls on us to affirm that our substance use is out of control, and that our lives have become chaotic as a result. Only with this acknowledgment can we move forward with a solution.

Acceptance then becomes the foundation to later recovery. There's even a famous passage in the Big Book of Alcoholics Anonymous about it:

And acceptance is the answer to all my problems today. When I am disturbed, it is because I find some person, place, thing or situation—some fact of my life—unacceptable to me. I can find no serenity until I accept that person, place, thing, or situation as being exactly the way it is supposed to be at this moment. Nothing, absolutely nothing, happens in God's world by mistake. Until I could accept my alcoholism, I could not stay sober; unless I accept life completely on life's terms, I cannot be happy. I need to concentrate not so much on what needs to be changed in the world as on what needs to be changed in me and my attitudes.

I have found that a lot of my clients' issues boil down to problems with acceptance or expectations. So often, the client wants to focus on what in their environment, or their partner, or their boss, needs to change in order to make their lives better.

Similarly, a lot of my students' struggles with clients come down to the same issue. The student wants to figure out how to change their client, to make them more compliant, more motivated, to make them do what they're asking them to do. It's common for me to ask both client and student what would be different if they were to totally accept what was going on—not focusing on what needs to change, but instead accepting the situation exactly as it is. *What would happen, I ask, if you were to let go of trying to make them different and instead radically accepted them as they are?* Asking them the radical acceptance question brings the focus inward, on what is happening inside of them.

I've been surprised by how quickly people can change once they turn this focus inward.

"Well, I guess I'd have to feel more empathy for the client. What they are being asked to do is really hard."

"I'd have to let go of trying to control my boss. She is who she is and I have to work with that."

When I redirect the conversation along this line, amazing things happen. Students find compassion for the struggles of their clients, and gain the ability to connect with them on a deeper level. And this is the level where true healing happens. Clients gain a freedom that allows them to move toward a solution. They put down the rope they are playing tug-of-war with and start thinking about what must change in them in order to chart a course forward. Asking this question, and shifting this focus really is one of the greatest tools in my counselor tool bag.

Wounded 10

Start . . . and Stop

As I suspected would happen, my counselor called the next afternoon. I didn't answer, but she left a message saying I had two hours to contact her; otherwise, she would send the police for a wellness check. I knew she was serious.

I was utterly, totally defeated. I no longer cared what happened to me. I no longer cared what anyone thought. I no longer wanted to invent some cover story, wiggle, and manipulate my way out of the latest hole. I was without any desire—to live or to die. I was in a land even beyond despair, where nothing existed.

I called her back. In a monotone, I told her about my use, my tampered drug test, and my suicide attempt. She recommended I go to a local emergency room immediately.

I asked a friend who was in early recovery to drive me over. I gave the hospital staff there a careful accounting of all the drugs I had taken. They ran a number of tests to determine the severity of the damage to my body. I tested positive for a number of drugs. I had blurry vision, nausea, and a headache, but otherwise my EKG and lab work all returned normal results. The ER doctor expressed surprise and even disbelief of my results, given the amount of pills I had taken. I had no explanation for the normal results. I was admitted to the psychiatric ward.

The morning after I was admitted, I met with a psychiatrist for an in-depth assessment. I gave my complete mental health history, along with an accounting of all the psychiatric medications I had tried over the years with little success. For some reason, she began to suspect that maybe I didn't have unipolar depression, but rather bipolar depression. I knew that in bipolar depression, the individual experiences depressive episodes, but they also have periods of mania or hypomania wherein they feel very good. I had absolutely no symptoms of this—no happy episodes. I had only experienced one continuous depressive state since childhood. She told me she wanted to conduct an experiment. She wanted to try me on a medication for bipolar depression, and see if I responded to that. She indicated that we would know in a day if it would work. I was surprised to learn this, as I knew most antidepressants took weeks to become effective.

I took the medication at bedtime. The next morning, I woke up early, alone in my room. As I opened my eyes and looked around the hospital room, I realized that I did indeed feel different. The first thing that hit me is I noticed colors again. I saw blues and greens and reds. Everything around me had been so grey for so long. I was suddenly interested in what was happening around me.

As I got up and moved to the common room of the ward, I also became aware that I didn't feel depressed or suicidal at all. When I thought about killing myself, it just seemed like the most ridiculous idea in the world. It seemed just as silly as asking someone to walk around with a ham on their head. I no longer felt depressed. *The psychiatrist was right; the experiment worked*, I thought. I was floored. I had never had this response to any medication for depression in the two decades I had been trying. I felt like I had a new lease on life.

The medication was very sedating for a couple of hours after I took it. I had to take it three times a day; after each dose, I would lay down for a nap for an hour or two, but otherwise would describe my mood as great. I remained in the hospital for two more days to adjust the dosing, but was released that Friday in time to go on an NA weekend retreat.

When I went to the psychiatric ward, I was discharged from my outpatient treatment because of my suicide attempt. They recommended to a higher level of care. I went to another substance use disorder assessment, and they recommended I attend a two-week day treatment program with lodging. I went, and felt stable and like I was making progress.

That summer, I was sincerely focused on sobriety. I honestly wanted to be sober. I was placed on long-term disability from work. I went to meetings most days, I met regularly with my sponsor to work the steps, and I attended therapy and psychiatry appointments. I remained abstinent from all substances.

I also felt ready to address my eating disorder. One of the recommendations made by my treatment team at Caron was for me to seek further treatment for my binge eating disorder, as it had become clear that I was still experiencing disordered eating. When I returned home, I contacted a local treatment center that specialized in treating eating disorders, and I went in for an assessment. I was recommended to an outpatient program that met for three hours a week for 16 weeks that summer. I enrolled when I came home from the day treatment program.

The program used a manualized cognitive behavioral treatment for binge eating disorders. I joined a group of about 10 people, all with the same binge eating disorder diagnosis, and we progressed through the treatment together. The treatment combined lectures and groups on topics like the mechanics of a binge eating disorder, body image, self-esteem, and cognitive distortions around weight and eating, with physical activity/body awareness segments and nutrition education. Each group included a catered meal where we all had to eat dinner together and tackle things like comfort foods, take-out, and celebratory meals. I was introduced to the concept of mindful eating, which I took to like a duck in water.

Mindful eating focuses on paying attention to our body's cues for hunger and satiety, and providing our bodies with foods that make it feel good. This means no foods are off limits, and that it's okay to trust our bodies to tell us what it needed. Mindful eating also encourages the eater to be fully present with the meal, to look and notice all the sensations that are associated with eating from a non-judgmental place. We notice how the food looks, smells, and tastes, and what our bodies feel as we chew and swallow each bite.

Most binge eaters eat very mindlessly. We really aren't present with our food. A binge is all about shoveling in food, bite after bite, in an attempt to numb the body and mind. So mindful eating was a complete 180 from that.

I also learned that I had been engaging in a self-reinforcing cycle of restriction and bingeing, and that my belief in "good" foods and "bad" foods was actually increasing my bingeing behaviors. I remember when I visited the cafeteria of the treatment center during my assessment. I saw they had Froot Loops cereal and Mountain Dew in their offerings. I was flabbergasted that a treatment center for eating disorders would actually be allowing their patients to eat such forbidden foods. That had not at all been my experience when I went to Rader at age 17. There, our menu was all low-fat, low-calorie foods. This time, when I shamefully admitted to my assessor that I started each morning by drinking a Mountain Dew, she non-judgmentally responded, "Perhaps your body needs the sugar first thing in the morning." I had never received anything but shaming messages regarding what I ate from any doctors or treatment providers, so this take was shocking to me. But it started me on a new path with my relationship with food.

Over the course of the 16-week treatment, I restructured my relationship with food. As part of the mindfulness, I was taught to become familiar with my body's cues for hunger and fullness. We had to rate our sense of hunger and fullness before and after every meal on a scale of 1 to 10, and we were encouraged to seek food when we dropped to a 3, and to try to stop eating when we reached a 7. Paradoxically, restricting my intake until I was starving myself to a level 1 was what had fueled the binges wherein I ate to a 10.

The treatment program was an adherent of the Healthy at Any Size movement, which uncoupled beliefs that weight was the sole determinant of health. This was where I was introduced to the research that questioned the long-held medical opinion that all fat people were unhealthy and all skinny people were healthy. In short, this four-month treatment blew apart everything I had ever been told or taught by family members, society, and doctors my whole life.

I found the group aspects of the treatment particularly helpful. To talk to other women who had the same beliefs and behaviors that I did, and to work with them to process this new way of relating to food, was powerful.

One of our meals was structured to be composed of eating nothing but forbidden foods. We each had to give a list of three to four forbidden foods to the dietician, who then provided a buffet of them toward the end of our treatment. On that day, I stood among the women looking at the foods and feeling so hesitant to approach them. We felt like we were doing something wrong, and this was made even worse because we were engaging in this eating behavior in public. The dieticians and counselors helped us walk through our emotions and beliefs about even engaging in the meal, and helped us internalize a belief that there were no such things as forbidden foods.

Another reason this treatment was such a radical departure for me was because, for over eight years, I had been a member of Overeaters Anonymous, which operated under very different beliefs. Because OA is a 12-step program, it includes a strong focus on the concept of abstinence, which OA defines a very particular way. Abstinence is the core goal for all 12-step programs. It's pretty easy to see how abstinence from alcohol or mood-altering substances can be defined and observed, but all of us have to eat, so defining abstinence here gets a little murky. Most of the OA groups I went to defined abstinence as sticking to an eating plan. OA members were encouraged to identify the exact foods they were going to eat at defined meals the next day, write them down, and call in the plan to their sponsor. Some OA groups even go so far as requiring exact weights and measures of food, and avoiding sugars and refined flour. In this way, abstinence meant you only ate what was on your food plan. There has been a redefinition in recent years to focus on the absence of compulsive behaviors around food, but when I was a member, this was the general principle people adhered to. It never worked for me. It felt like replacing one compulsion (to binge) with another (to hyper-control food intake).

But what this new treatment was teaching me resonated deeply. To listen to my body, and trust its guidance, was a radical departure from all previous attempts to address my eating disorder. To stop measuring my success by my weight, shape, and size. To focus on helping and caring for my body so that I could do the physical things I wanted to do.

And it worked. Since that treatment, I have been in full remission from my eating disorder. I have made peace with food, and am no longer a slave to it. I have still gone through periods of time when I have difficulty with mindful eating, but I no longer binge. I am forever grateful for the treatment team who worked with me, and I have shifted my professional practice toward such principles with the clients I work with.

Healing 17

Inner Child Work

About two years into my personal therapy work with Peggy, she introduced the concept of inner child work. At this point, I had been attending 12-step groups for about six months, and while there were no changes in my eating behaviors, I had found a group of people who I felt understood me. But I was still extremely depressed and bingeing daily. Over the years, I had heard people every now and then mention this thing called their inner child, but I dismissed it as some kind of new age fad. I was beginning my fourth year of graduate study in psychology, and it hadn't been mentioned in any of my classes.

So when Peggy brought it up, I was skeptical. But I trusted her enough to follow her advice at this point. She pointed me toward the work of Alice Miller, and her book *The Drama of the Gifted Child*. In this book, Dr. Miller describes a theory that some children are born *"gifted,"* particularly wired to be more sensitively attuned to the desires and needs of other people. When they encounter a situation where their emotional needs aren't being met, they adopt the needs and desires of the caregivers in their lives. Then they seek to find achievement and success in order to find approval and love and get those unmet emotional needs met. This sensitivity and achievement are the gifted parts of the gifted child. But in order to achieve this, the child must suppress their own emotional reactions, needs, and expressions. This leads to the child developing into an adult who, while achieving much in life, nevertheless is depressed because they are cut off from their inner experience. The solution, Miller says, is to uncover and rediscover all those hidden, suppressed childhood feelings and experiences.

As I digested the material in the book and processed it in therapy, I could certainly see myself in the description of the gifted child. I was very success-oriented, and had achieved a lot academically. After all, I was in a doctoral program in psychology. I recognized that in my life, I was able to attend especially well to the thoughts, needs, and desires of others. I seemed to be particularly good at reading and autopsying other peoples' thoughts and motives.

And I was definitely cut off from my childhood. Whenever I told stories about my childhood, I felt no emotional connection to the stories at all. It was as if I were conveying the stories of other people. When I imagined my childhood selves at different ages, it was like they were separate people, independent of my body and mind.

My initial skepticism was lessening. *Okay*, I thought, *maybe there is something to this stuff.*

After I experienced some initial buy-in to this theory, Peggy helped me design a process to begin getting in touch with my own inner child. I was to spend time in meditation, emptying my mind of outside intrusions, and imagining that I was in a room with my inner child. I was to do this several times a week, in between my therapy sessions. At some point, she told me some version of me as a child would appear. We didn't know what age she would be, or under what circumstances she would be in. I was instructed to trust the process, and keep my focus on being open and accepting of whatever unfolded.

It started very slowly. Interestingly, during my first meditation session, as I was imagining sitting in an empty room, an upholstered brown chair appeared across the room. I recognized it immediately. It was the brown chair that sat in our living room when I was a child. Slowly, over a few meditation sessions, I was able to realize that my two-year-old self was hiding behind the chair. This was interesting to me, because as a child, I often ran and hid behind this chair. It was set in a corner, so there was a little niche behind it. It was too small for an adult to fit in, but it was perfect for my two-year-old body. I remember hiding behind it when I wanted to get away from everyone.

One time when I was three, my parents were hosting a gathering, and I didn't feel anyone was paying attention to me. I went to my hiding place behind the chair and waited for someone to notice and come looking for me so I could get some attention. But no one noticed I was gone. Finally, once all the guests had left, my parents noticed I was missing and started looking. I thought they were going to be mad if they found out I had intentionally hidden for so long, so I pretended to be asleep instead.

For the first six months of my meditations, my two-year-old self stubbornly remained hidden behind the brown chair. Peggy coached me to simply remain seated across the imaginary room, and focus on opening myself up to accepting the child's need to remain hidden. And so I tried to do this. It was frustrating at first. I felt an inner demand to call the child to me, to force her from behind the chair. Then I wanted to get up from my seat and walk behind the chair so I could see her. I worked over time to let go of those desires, and meditated on being open, not wishing the child would appear and come to me, but sending out feelings of love and acceptance to the room, hoping that she would pick up on them.

And then one day, she popped her head out from behind the chair and looked at me. I felt stunned. My real breath quickened. I could see an apprehensive look on her face, but also one of curiosity. She smiled and giggled, and then disappeared behind the chair again. When I reported this to Peggy, she said this was wonderful progress and to really dig into this work right then.

Over the course of the next few weeks, my inner two-year-old slowly emerged from behind the chair. She still wouldn't come to me, but she felt safe enough to play about in the room. In my meditations, imaginary toys would appear too, and she would play with them. I could sense she knew I was in the room, and she would occasionally look over at me, but she was more focused on the toys. Peggy instructed me to remain in my imaginary chair, while focusing on feeling open and accepting. So that's what I did.

Then one day, my inner two-year-old approached me with arms outstretched, holding a toy. She wanted to show me the toy and share it with me. I could feel my real heartbeat increase. I took a deep breath and exhaled. In my meditation, I opened my arms and smiled. She stopped at my feet and thrust the toy into my lap. She wasn't ready to climb onto my lap, but stood and talked to me about the toy. I focused on remaining open, showing nothing but acceptance and curiosity. I listened to her. Then I spoke.

"Thank you for showing me the toy," I offered. I was glowing inside. She had finally acknowledged me and showed interest in me.

The milestones kept coming. Soon, she asked to sit in my lap. I imagined picking her up and placing her sideways across my legs. At first, she always brought a toy to share or play with. I focused on always being positive and encouraging, praising her for all that she was sharing and doing. Then one day, she came empty-handed. I placed her on my lap, and we just spent time together. I could sense in her a growing comfort with me. I could tell she wasn't ready for a hug, but she was enjoying the time she spent with me. She always remained upright and facing me.

Finally, after six months behind the chair, and then two months playing and sharing, one day she relaxed her body and leaned into me. I placed my arms around her and pulled her in. We just sat there in silence, feeling the closeness. I could feel her little body, curved and tucked into mine. She was warm and totally relaxed. I focused on making my body equally relaxed.

This whole time, I had been imagining myself sitting in a stiff dining room chair in the corner of the room. Now, I began to imagine myself sitting in the brown chair, with her in my lap.

We spent weeks just cuddling—for many hours at a time. I held her close and snuggled in, leaning back in the chair to put us more into a lying position. I focused on sending only positive energy and acceptance toward her, and reinforced this by telling her she was wonderful and delightful.

By now, I was having glimpses of her in my real life. Something would happen, and I would occasionally feel something that felt like two-year-old joy, or curiosity, or anger. I focused on just noticing these events, and letting the emotions flow through me. I noticed that these feelings, while they felt like a two-year-old's, were very much coming from within me. I could picture my two-year-old self, but now she felt internal, instead of the separate person I had recollected before I started this process. And when I felt any two-year-old feelings, I treated them with acceptance. "Yes," I told my inner two-year-old self, "That is exactly what you are feeling. And that is the exact right feeling to have." I would listen to the feeling that was in response to a real-life, real-time event, and affirm and respond to it.

I have to admit that the whole process felt weird to me. Not as weird and unbelievable as astrology or tarot cards were, but something like fortune-telling weird. This was not the kind of training I was receiving in my doctoral program. So far, I had done almost two years of placements in two different Midwest college counseling centers. I did a lot of interpersonal work, as most of the college students experienced difficulty forming friendships and romantic relationships. I worked with a lot of depression and anxiety too. But I wasn't talking to anyone about inner children or conducting any mindful meditations with them. I was being trained to deliver mostly brief interventions, usually six sessions or less. As students, we were allowed to carry one or two clients the full year, but even with them, I wasn't doing this deep work. I did a lot of cognitive behavioral work, teaching clients about the connection between their thoughts and their feelings and actions.

At the same time, I had to admit that this process was having a very powerful effect on me. It was working. I was indeed uncovering hidden old emotions and selves. I was feeling more connected to my childhood.

As I made progress, I didn't have to do the meditations as deeply or as intentionally as I did at first. Now, pretty much anywhere I was, I could just focus inward, and my two-year-old self would appear. Sometimes I could imagine her with me in the room wherever I was, doing whatever I was doing. She came to class with me, and showed up at my 12-step meetings. When I spent time with friends, she would be there. The only time she would never appear was when I was with any family member.

I would sometimes see a sister, or my mom, for a weekend visit. I became aware that during these visits, my two-year-old self was completely inaccessible. I brought this up to Peggy, and she responded that I should simply trust that the two-year-old me did not feel comfortable with her family members, and had chosen to remain hidden. So I did.

Over the next decade and a half, my inner child grew up within me. I spent about nine months becoming intimately acquainted with my two-year-old, and then I noticed she was getting older. I began to see myself as a four- and five-year-old. These inner children were in my current life, and I could regularly feel them within me. In my meditations, I experienced the thrill of starting kindergarten. I also had memories of playing in our backyard around that age, which butted up against a small swamp. In this swamp one day, we discovered a Venus flytrap, which are native only to the small coastal area I lived in. We dug it up and brought it inside and tried to feed it. It didn't live. I recalled how sad this had made me.

For my inner four- and five-year-olds, I did the same thing that I had done with my two-year-old. I would imagine spending time with them, and giving them praise and love. I would imagine listening to them, and hug them; oh, we did lots of hugging and cuddling. I had learned that my job in this whole exercise was to be the parent to myself that I had always needed. To provide the unconditional love and comfort. To be steady and true. And above all, to fully see and accept the child.

Then a gap appeared. The next me to show up was seven years old. Even now, the ages of late five to middle seven remain a blank space in my inner experience. Peggy would tell me that this must have been a time of great distress, and that I could only trust the process and that at some point in my life, she might show up, but maybe never.

But my inner seven-year-old . . . boy, she was fun. Bursting with curiosity and energy. She liked being involved in everything. She liked cooking and making a mess. She loved learning new things, especially science. She loved playing make-believe. Even today, the most enduring inner image of myself as a seven-year-old is me standing tall, hands on hips, with a towel tied around my neck, playing superhero and running and jumping over all the furniture. And she was full of confidence. There was nothing she couldn't do. No adventure she didn't feel prepared for. Like I said, she was a lot of fun. And she wasn't interested in hugs or cuddles. She wanted a partner in her adventures. And so that's what we did.

A few years later was a different story. When my inner child had progressed to the age of 10, something different appeared. A withdrawn, quiet girl. She didn't make a lot of eye contact, and generally kept her head down. She had begun an early puberty a year before, the first in her class, and was developing an adult female body. She was uncomfortable in this body, and with the different attention she had begun getting because of it. Depression hung like an invisible cloud all around her.

In real life, I had begun gaining weight at this age, which also drew negative attention from my parents. Food had become the only comfort I felt. Clothes had become tight. I vividly remember that I used to stand in the evening sun, and as the setting sun stretched my shadow into a long thin person, I would try and pinpoint which set of elongated thin legs I wished I had.

Reparenting this child involved a whole different set of skills. With her, my job was to just be present with her and her pain. Here, the imaginary meditation sessions were spent sitting with her side-by-side on a couch, talking. I spent hours explaining to her what was happening with her body. She wasn't comfortable telling me her experiences, but I talked to her as if I understood them anyway. I affirmed her reactions and feelings, and told her they were a perfectly normal reaction to what she was going through. I told her that it made sense she felt uncomfortable about the sexual attention she was receiving; it was indeed uncomfortable to be looked at this way as a child. I sat with her in her pain—not judging it, not repressing it or trying to change it. Just affirming that I saw it and was there to hold it with her. I was gentle with her in speech, but overflowing with love and acceptance.

Over the weeks and months we spent together, I could see she began to feel better. She lifted her head more and looked at me as she spoke, and the fog of depression that enveloped her lessened.

Twelve-year-old me showed up the next year and was overflowing with anger. When we spent time together, she sat with her arms folded on the other side of the couch, silent. When she made eye contact, she shot daggers of hatred from her eyes. She was angry with everything. In real life, this was the year I skipped from sixth to eighth grade and received all the negative attention from my new classmates. Before she showed up, if you had asked me about what I remembered from this age, I would have described a deeply depressed, full-of-despair adolescent. Anger was not in my memory. But boy, was she full of it.

This makes sense to me now. I was horrifically bullied, and no adult did anything. It wasn't safe to share any of my experiences with my parents; any expression of negative feelings was quickly shut down by them. I had learned anger was not an acceptable feeling to have, so I stuffed it deep down.

So this time, I just let the anger fill the room. At first, I didn't say much. I think she just needed someone to see her anger and not try and push it down or away. As I meditated, I relaxed my body and imagined opening my soul to take in all the anger that was in the room—but in a way that didn't judge it or try to change it. At the same time, I sent out feelings of acceptance into the room, not to crowd out the anger, but to join it. After some time, she became comfortable enough to start talking. My meditation sessions shifted, and now I imagined myself talking with her, reflecting everything that was happening to her and explaining why she was feeling this really appropriate anger. And as we spent time talking and seeing the anger, it, too, began to lessen, just as her earlier depression had lessened.

This inner child work has gone on now for almost two decades. Generally, every few years, a slightly older version of my childhood self would appear, and I would spend a few weeks or months working through all the feelings and reactions of each age. As they healed, these inner children joined me in my daily life. When something would happen, I would have my adult reaction, but occasionally, an older feeling would surface from an earlier version of me. I became comfortable with these experiences, and just let them happen. The good feelings would surface too. When I was discovering some new place, my inner seven-year-old would join me and delight in the adventure.

This work continues today in my recovery. A couple of years ago, my inner 16-year-old showed up. I wasn't expecting her. I was going about my daily life, and suddenly developed an intense interest and fascination with both Billie Eilish and the Jonas Brothers. Most would agree that these are two musical genres that don't go together at all. Billie Eilish is totally emo, all depression and angst. The Jonas Brothers are all about fun and happy emotions. But I was driven to create a playlist that blended songs from each of them. I listened to this playlist almost nonstop, mostly in my car. One song would be full of angst, and the next would explode with joy and excitement. I felt driven to watch all the music videos that went with these songs. I even watched all the documentaries about both Eilish and the Brothers. Multiple times. My wife was totally bewildered but thoroughly amused. And then one day I finally realized, this was my inner 16-year-old showing up. Now the playlist made sense; this is exactly the kind of music she would listen to. I began to have imaginary meditation sessions in my car. My 16-year-old would appear in the passenger seat, and we began to talk. Of course the adolescent me would be more comfortable talking in a car!

This inner me was all about experiencing all her emotions. That's why she called on Billie Eilish and the Jonas Brothers. And her emotions were intensely felt—anger, joy, despair—one after the other, embedded in the songs. She wanted each emotion to fill the car as we drove. We steeped in them and let them ooze out the windows. The adult psychologist me knows this was developmentally appropriate. Part of adolescence involves experiencing emotions more intensely than at any other time in life. The teenage brain is wired this way to undergo a period of intense development. During this phase, the limbic system is very active, and connections to the prefrontal cortex are less than they will be as an adult. The limbic system is the seat of emotions, and the prefrontal cortex is where higher order rational thinking occurs. This makes teenagers' brains produce massive, overriding emotions that dominate their experience. And boy, was that evident in my inner 16-year-old.

Once we felt all the emotions, our conversations shifted. This 16-year-old was full of questions about life. She craved guidance on transitioning to an adult. She wanted to know about applying to college, and how to manage money. This made sense to the adult me. When I was in high school, I never got a lot of guidance on things like this. My life was pretty rocky for two decades past my adolescence. So I would imagine myself as the parent, and as we drove around listening to music (at a much lower volume), I instructed her on life lessons like these.

I don't know how many more of these inner me's will show up in the future. But I've gotten comfortable with the process of what to do when they appear.

All my earlier skepticism about the theory of the inner child is gone. Now that I'm a psychologist, I've worked to become academically familiar with the theory, how this treatment works, and how to counsel someone through it. It's become something I've employed with some clients I've worked with. By no means do I think this type of therapy is for everyone. But for clients whose presenting concerns connect back to difficult childhoods, it works pretty well. And not all clients want to do this work. When I've determined that it might be an appropriate treatment, I explain the theory and what this work looks like to the client. I then communicate that the client has the choice of whether or not to go down this path. Like me, most clients express skepticism at this treatment, which I say is normal. Some clients decide not to do this, and like any treatment, it would be unethical to force them into it, so we find a different path through their pain. But for the ones who do choose to go forward, I find this very gratifying work to do with a client. It's a great treatment for any member of the phenomenal women's club, talked about earlier in this book.

One client, who was a member of the club, met with me for a couple of years on and off. She expressed a pretty strong disbelief that this treatment would work, but consented to trying it. I gave her the homework I had been given, and often during our sessions, I would help her visualize her inner, younger self and coach her on how to interact with this self. The client never talked much about the homework, and I didn't press the issue, mindful of her initial doubt. But when we got to the end of her time with me, we reflected on the work she had done. I asked her what was the most impactful event or thing that she experienced in her work, and she surprised me by saying it was the inner child work. I laughed with delight and commented on her initial disbelief. She laughed along with me, and said she agreed that she was a hard customer around this, but darn it, it really did work for her.

Now that I'm a counselor educator, responsible for training the next generation of therapists, I often reflect back on my own lack of training on this. Still now, this theory is not taught as part of most core curriculums. Most curriculums have a specific class on different psychological theories. Students study about a dozen of the most common counseling theories, starting with Freud's psychanalytic theory and then moving on to others, including Roger's person-centered approach, Beck's cognitive theory, Eptson and White's narrative therapy, Klerman and Weissman's interpersonal theory, and several modern theories. While the inner child work is most closely linked with more modern psychoanalytic theory, it's not taught as part of the theory at all. I sometimes bring it in when I'm supervising students on clinical placements, when there is more leeway for teaching this kind of stuff. It remains some of my favorite work to teach and practice.

Healing 18

Body Gratitude

About two years after I got gastric bypass surgery, I decided to go to a support group for people who had had the same surgery. This was just after getting home from my treatment at Caron. I was trying to get sober and thought that this group might be a good idea, as I still struggled with food. The surgical program I had used offered a monthly support group for people waiting for the surgery or for those post-surgery who struggled in any way. The group met in a conference room in the hospital where I'd had the surgery for 90 minutes once a month.

I came and took a seat near the door. The group was moderated by a health care professional, but there was no agenda. People just started talking. Many shared on the struggles they'd had since their surgeries. Losing weight had created saggy bodies, and people shared they felt they were ugly. Some shared that the weight wasn't coming off as fast as they wanted, or their relationships had changed since they became smaller. Their spouses were jealous of the newfound attention they were receiving. I sat there and listened, but I realized I was having a very different experience.

About halfway through, I decided to share. My 12-step recovery programming kicked in. Everything I learned in the rooms of Overeater's Anonymous came flowing out of me. I shared about how grateful I was for my body, for how it had survived everything I had put it through. For decades, I had treated it poorly. I gave it mounds of unhealthy food. I stuffed my body over and over again until it was in pain. I made it purge through vomiting and laxatives. I had taken thousands and thousands of drugs that had damaged it. And yet, it had survived. In fact, I marveled at what my body had been through. Through all of its abuse, I had never developed diabetes. Even with all the drugs and alcohol I had consumed, I never once had anything more than mildly elevated liver enzymes. Hell, I had tried to kill my body on several occasions. But my body withstood all of this. It was strong. My body was amazing. I was so lucky to have my body.

I also shared that I knew the fat I had accumulated served a purpose. I was afraid of other people, and my fat protected me in this way. Because most of society is repelled by fat people, it made it easier to maintain an isolated existence. I thanked my body for taking care of me during this time, until I was ready to engage with other people.

I'd also come to understand that part of what made my body so hardy was my ancestors. I come from a long line of poor farmers and fishermen who lived a poverty subsistence. As a result, they evolved metabolisms that were very good at squeezing every drop of energy from its food, because food was scarce. I inherited that metabolism. My body was a marvelous, efficient, machine.

As I shared all of this, it was clear the other participants had never heard someone talk about her body that way. The moderator thanked me for sharing, and privately shared that she was grateful I had this point of view, as this was rarely shared by group participants but sorely needed.

The truth is, I learned most of this in OA meetings, listening to other members express gratitude for their bodies. Over the years, this viewpoint had finally sunk in. I never really knew this until that day at the support group. It turns out OA never did help me heal my issues with food, but it did a lot to heal my relationship with my body.

Despite these incredible changes to my relationship with my body, I would still struggle with the appearance of parts of my body for years to come. I stored a lot of my extra weight in my belly, arms, and thighs. Losing the weight created a massively droopy abdomen. It was the body part I had the most shame with. It bothered me so much I decided to have plastic surgery to remove it. For decades, I rarely wore pants because of how my belly looked in them. Removing it did allow me to fit more comfortably in some clothes. But even to this day, I sometimes look at my flabby upper arms and thighs with disgust. I vacillate between working on accepting and loving these parts of myself, and thinking about getting more plastic surgery. For now, I've decided to hold off on any decision.

Since that time, I've worked with many clients with body image issues. Very rarely does a client not have them, thanks to living in US society. I can easily say it has come up with virtually every client. When it does, I give them a homework assignment to practice some body gratitude. I have them make a list of everything their bodies have done. All the life it has created, all the harm it has suffered, all the ways it has survived. If the client has struggled with weight, I ask them to list the ways their fat protected them. I then ask the client to read each statement and say out loud, "I am grateful for my body." For most clients, this is an entirely different way to look at their bodies.

Most clients struggle with engaging with this assignment. They are so disconnected from any positive relationship with their bodies. But I have found that any clients with a regular exercise or yoga routine seem to have less trouble. And sometimes moms can immediately share gratitude that their bodies were able to create life, but they find little to like besides that. But for clients who are able to do this assignment, they share that it really helped them see how they had so many hidden shame messages about their bodies that were connected to so many aspects of their lives.

Wounded 11

Stuck

As the summer wore on, I recognized that I needed to return to work. At the time, as I've stated, Minnesota had a law that all clinicians working in treatment centers must be "free from chemical use problems" for two years. Since I no longer met that requirement, returning to clinical work at this time was not a possibility. I had lost my job as a mental health practitioner.

However, in addition to its treatment centers, Hazelden also operated a graduate school that trained addiction counselors. I had a fair amount of teaching experience, having taught high school for two years and several college classes while I was in graduate school. I had even received an award for my teaching. So I applied for a faculty opening at Hazelden. Because it was at a different location, my use was not known to the selection committee. I got the job and started working again that August. Overall, my life was on a good path.

The unravelling started innocently enough. At the end of the summer, I was meeting with my psychiatrist for a routine medication review. In addition to the medication I started taking in the hospital, I was also prescribed another medication to treat tremors, a common side effect of the first medication. Ever so casually, the psychiatrist asked if I had ever abused this tremor medication. I felt the addict part of my brain light up immediately. *Wait,* I thought, *you can abuse this drug? I've been taking something that I could possibly get high on?* I kept my cool and honestly responded that no, I had never abused this drug.

But the seed was planted.

What most non-addicts have a hard time understanding is just how all-consuming an obsession to use can become. Once an idea to use—even the slightest sliver of a thought—takes hold, it hijacks all cognitive functioning. It grows exponentially until nothing else exists. From a tiny little ember, a raging inferno arises.

Once I learned that it was possible to experience mind-altering effects by taking more of the tremor medication than prescribed, I could think of little else. I knew it was not a substance that would show up on my random urine screens for my monitoring program, which had been my main deterrent to using.

I decided to try it out.

It wasn't a pleasant high by a long shot, but it was enough to take me out of the present moment. I started getting high on it a couple of times a month.

After a few months, I graduated to abusing diphenhydramine, a common antihistamine most widely known as Benadryl. Again, it was a fairly nasty high, but after taking several dozen, it can induce hallucinations and extreme altered-ness. I wasn't being tested for this drug either.

It wasn't until a few years later that I fully understood what led to this return to use. It didn't make much sense. I was doing well. But I had not learned to be comfortable in my own skin. Experiencing emotions, even positive emotions, was painful. And the highs supplied by these two medications, while unpleasant, felt better than being fully present in my body.

For about a year, it was something I only did a couple of times a month. I was full of shame over my use, but felt I could not reach out to anyone for help. Because I was in a monitoring program, if I told one person—my therapist, my sponsor, my psychiatrist—I would be reported, and then everyone would know. Ironically, the tool that was supposed to support my recovery (monitoring) actually hindered it. So I kept my secret hidden from everyone and pretended to be someone with growing sobriety time.

I wasn't a very good professor that first year. I did the bare minimum and stayed under the radar.

Part of my position involved managing clinical placements for our graduate students. Our students were required to obtain 880 hours of clinical field experience as part of their degree. Many of these students interned at my old facility, requiring me to interact with staff there as well. Each interaction was excruciating for me because of the amount of shame I felt over how I'd left. But I can say everyone was incredibly kind. Most only knew that I had left suddenly and were just concerned if I was okay. I didn't understand why they weren't all judging me; surely they thought I was a horrible person. But when I had to visit the site in my capacity as clinical placements coordinator, people's faces brightened when they saw me. I received many hugs. Still, I didn't feel the caring at all—only the shame.

I maintained my occasional using pattern until the spring. After each use, I would feel a real, sincere desire to be sober. But the ember was still there, and it would grow over the course of a few days until I relented.

I met with my therapist and sponsor weekly and lied about my use.

I submitted my quarterly reports to the monitoring program indicating everything was fine. I went to four to five meetings a week and played a sober person. I would volunteer to lead meetings or maintain the phone list. I even served as my home group's representative to the area level, where people from all the meetings came together once a month to handle administrative tasks and make decisions about any changes.

I maintained this life for over a year.

The next spring, I decided that I wanted to start dating again. It had been five years since I'd been in a relationship, and I was lonely. Underneath this desire was a belief that this would motivate me to stay sober. One of my strongest values was to not involve other people in my addiction. I had seen what addiction did to family members. I was determined not to do this. So I self-imposed a three-month period of abstinence from all substances to prove I could do it. Successful, I went online and set up a profile on a dating website. After a few unexciting encounters with a few women, I met Sarah for coffee. She seemed interesting. We messaged each other for a few days, and then arranged another date.

As I got to know her, something weird happened. I truly enjoyed spending time with her. I felt good when I was with her. But as soon as I drove away, another feeling would settle in. My mind would dredge up all the things that were wrong about her. As I thought about these really petty things, I would feel a strong aversion to her. I would formulate a plan to stop seeing her. But then she would ask for another date, and for some reason I would go. Again, I would enjoy myself and getting to know her. I was introduced to her family, who lived locally. And each time I left, my mind would fixate on her flaws.

It was much later when I figured out what was happening. I was encountering a knock-down, drag-out fight with my own psyche. All the things I was judgmental about Sarah were traits that I judged about myself. The hate I was projecting onto her was really about my deep shame for my own flaws. The judgment I felt of her was really my self-judgement projected. My subconscious mind was battling itself. And the fight was epic. I imagined it as a large, all-consuming cloud surrounding me, reaching high up into the sky, blocking out all light.

Sarah and I continued dating a couple of times a week for a couple of months. Our relationship became physical.

That summer, she suggested we plan a weekend getaway. It would be our first overnight trip together. I was hesitant but agreed. I had never been to Fargo, North Dakota, and mentioned this to her. She thought it was hilarious that someone would *want* to go to Fargo for a vacation, but she was game to go. She booked a hotel for two nights, and that Fourth of July weekend, we went.

It was one of the best weekends of my life. We went to a local amusement park that had a mini-golf course. Both of us professed a love of mini-golf. To make the game more interesting, we bet that the loser would have to buy dinner that night. I won.

That night, we went to a local diner, and she had to buy me some of the best liver and onions I'd ever had. I delighted as Sarah expressed exaggerated disgust at my meal. We also bought fireworks and set them off in the hotel parking lot, running around like teenagers.

The hotel had a $1 blackjack table. I had never gambled regularly, but had inherited my mother's love for blackjack. We sat at the table and had a great time interacting with the dealer and other players. I ended up winning $20.

Something different was definitely happening. I was having fun. Sarah was wonderful to be with. All the demon aversion thoughts I had been having were gone. I was falling in love.

We returned home to Minneapolis that Monday. At this point, we were spending most evenings together.

Two days later, Sarah was gone to play softball with a team she'd been on for years, giving me a free evening. Incxplicably, I had a strong urge to drink a beer. I have no idea where the urge came from. Alcohol had never been something I had really used. I was strictly into pills. But in this moment, my frontal lobe was entirely shut off. My higher existence and consciousness were gone.

I drove to a nearby liquor store in this haze and bought a 40-ounce Budweiser. I came home and guzzled down the beer. As I sat the beer down on the counter, a swirl of thoughts and emotions returned. I was so perplexed as to what had just happened. *Why in the world would I do this? What was happening to me?*

My body had quite a reaction to the alcohol. Within minutes, my gut exploded and I could not get to the bathroom quickly enough. The diarrhea spilled out as I was pulling my pants down and soiled my underwear and pants, dripping down my leg. The violent reaction my body was having mirrored what was happening in my mind.

I put the soiled clothes in the washing machine and sat down on my couch. My consciousness slowly returned, and a deep shame welled up within me. *What I did was bad, horrible,* I told myself. I was deeply confused. But the one thing I knew for sure was that I had to hide this.

I got up the next morning and went about my day as if nothing had happened.

At this point, I had been in the monitoring program for two years. Part of my agreement was to submit to random drug screens. The monitoring program had assigned me two colors, yellow and purple, and I had to call a number every morning where they would announce what color was being called that day. For two weeks after my use, I held my breath each morning when I called to find out what the color of the day was.

Neither of my two colors were called any of the days. I was going to get away with it.

The shame I felt about my use was still unbearable, but I knew how to handle shame: you shove that shit down, deep down, and numb it with use. So when this *call to numb* would come, I began regularly using diphenhydramine again. I continued through the winter.

I chose diphenhydramine because it was cheap, readily available, and not part of my drug screens. I could get 100 pills for about five bucks.

Diphenhydramine is categorized as an antihistamine, and it has two regular over-the-counter uses: as an anti-allergy treatment, and as a sleeping aid. Taking too much of it can produce some mild euphoria, feelings of excitement, and hallucinations.

I never really relished a diphenhydramine high the way I did opiates, but it did the job. For me, a typical use happened on the nights I wasn't with Sarah. I would usually ingest 50 to 70 pills over the course of two hours. It almost always produced a profound dissociative episode. I would have little awareness of what was happening around me, combined with an inability to control most of my motor movements. At the highest does, I would experience auditory hallucinations—in the form of voices indistinctly whispering behind me. Whenever this happened, I would feel a sense of relief and accomplishment. *Ah, yes, there they are, I'm definitely totally high now*, I reassured myself.

At such high doses, I was also putting myself at risk of an overdose, which I actually believe did happen a few times. I'm almost certain I experienced a seizure one night.

And so, the cycle was happening again. I was secretly spiraling into addiction, while functioning in my profession on the outside. My career as a professor was actually starting to take off. I was becoming known as an intelligent, talented educator who guided students into the art and science of the counseling profession. My student evaluations were off the charts. I started presenting at conferences and workshops. I started being sought after for consultations. I developed a popular lecture for patients, which I delivered once a month. And my relationship with Sarah continued to progress. I hid my use from her, and from my entire recovery community, continuing to present myself as someone with three years of sobriety.

And so, the two paths inside of me diverged again. The wounded part of me, which began to veer ever so slightly with the psychiatrist's question, continued to secretly turn toward pain, suffering, and addiction. And the healing part of me began a new journey, as a professor, and slowly curved toward recognition and success.

Healing 19

The Battle to Be

As stated earlier, one of the truisms that therapists have spouted for genera-tions is that we are *human beings*, not *human doings*. Almost universally, people come into therapy measuring their worth by what they do, and almost univer-sally, therapists remind clients that worth is inherent—no action required. I've found that most people have great difficulty with just being. And I've struggled mightily with this myself.

It blew my mind when Peggy explained this to me when I first started seeing her. The concept of inherent worth was beyond my understanding. This began my quest for being, which I've been working on now for nearly two decades.

One practice recommended for people working on this is to engage in mind-fulness meditation. In this practice, people sit (or stand, or lie) in silence and focus their attention on their breath—feeling the cool inhale hit the back of the throat, the lungs expanding, the lungs deflating, the warm exhalation. Inevitably, some outside thought will come into the mind. The goal is not to keep this from happening; rather, it is to notice when it is happening, to non-judgmentally allow the thought to come and go, and then to mindfully refocus on one's breath. After a beat or two, another outside thought will come, and again, the practice is to note it, not judge it, allow it to come and go, and come back to the breath.

There's a reason meditation is called a practice. No one does it perfectly. In fact, the goal is not to do it perfectly, but to train the body to let go of thoughts past and future, and to focus on the present moment.

It turns out this is excruciatingly difficult.

My first attempts were, to put it kindly, a real mess. I would find a quiet place in my house, put on a guided meditation, and turn my attention to my breath. *In and out. In and out.* At once, I became aware of the deluge of thoughts running rampant in my brain. All the things I needed to get done that day. *The trash needs to go out. I need to go to the store for bread. I need to finish writing that paper.* And then snippets of conversations from the morning or the night before would enter. A replay of a conversation I'd had with a professor. *I wonder what she meant when she said . . .? I need to call my mom.* My mind was nowhere near a quiet refuge; it was a superhighway packed with thoughts zooming by. The more I tried to quiet my mind, the louder the thoughts seemed to become. I gave up after a few minutes. I felt like a failure.

Later, I learned this is a very typical first attempt at mindfulness meditation. I continued to work on it over the next few years. I went to the local Zen center and engaged in zazen, a type of sitting meditation in Japanese Zen Buddhism.

When I started working with adolescents at one of Hazelden's facilities, I was the therapist leading the mindful meditations in weekly therapy groups. To aid younger minds, I added in the instructions to visualize sitting by a gently flowing river, and to see thoughts as leaves floating by. Again, the idea is to note the thought, but also allow it to float on by, always returning to the breath. The clients found it just as difficult as I did.

Over time, however, a practice slowly emerged. The trick, I learned, was not to try to have a blank mind. Rather it was to wholly accept whatever thought was there and not judge it, but not hold on and perseverate on it either. Not to try to not think, but to allow the thought to leave, always coming back to the breath.

In this way, I began to experience the present moment. Over time, I've been able to experience the present moment in whatever I'm doing: mindfully washing the dishes, or walking the dog. After some time, I realized that the tasks that I had always enjoyed most—teaching, counseling—were in fact enjoyed because I was doing these things mindfully. When I teach, I am fully present in the room with the students. I am completely focused on the lesson, completely connected to the students. I'm not having outside thoughts come in about what I need to do or what I did yesterday. When I'm sitting with a client, I can get to a state where my focus is entirely on just being with them—listening to them and engaging in conversation.

I've come to understand happiness and contentment only come when one is fully present. Being present is a prerequisite of happiness.

Part of the reason this is such an accomplishment for me is because, for years, my main coping skill was dissociation. Dissociation is the exact opposite of mindfulness. Dissociation occurs when a person disconnects from all thoughts and feelings, and becomes completely detached from experiencing the present moment. It is a mental strategy—often first developed in childhood—used by people when physical removal from a situation is not possible. It's common in childhood, because children usually have little ability to leave a situation or keep something from happening. When all else fails, they could go away in their minds to keep from experiencing something unpleasant or traumatic.

I was a champ at dissociating. Whenever anything got too intense, I could actually feel my body disconnecting, going away, and my mind floating away from the situation. It was such a common occurrence that I usually wasn't aware I was doing it. It was probably a daily practice for the first four decades of my life. I spent very little time experiencing the present moment.

One consequence of dissociation for me has been the lack of memories. When I'm dissociating, I'm not laying down memories, so often the most emotionally intense moments of my life, I have no memories of. Sometimes I've been grateful for this. I don't want to remember being raped, or being abused. But sometimes, not being able to remember bothers me.

The two times I completely unraveled in my NA group, disclosing my use and despair, I have no memory of. They are such pivotal moments of my life, but I don't remember them at all, because I was dissociated the whole time.

And it's not just painful memories I don't have. I would often dissociate during any emotionally intense moment. I don't have any memory of walking across the graduation stage for my doctorate, or defending and passing my dissertation. I don't remember national presentations I gave. I'm sad when I think about that.

As I progressed in my recovery, a funny thing started to happen. My ability to dissociate dissipated. Or, more accurately, my *need* to dissociate dissipated. I would find myself in emotional situations, but remaining present. Often, at the end of an intense day, I would be aware that I had remained present the whole time. It really was a new experience for me. The most eventful moment for me was my wedding, just two years into my sobriety. As the day approached, I could feel my excitement rising. I became afraid that the day was going to be so intense, I would dissociate and not experience it, leaving me with no memories of it. My only goal for the day was to be present. I talked about this fear for weeks in therapy leading up to the ceremony. Was the day going to be too intense for me?

My therapist listened, and she encouraged me to trust myself. If I was capable, I would remain present. There wasn't really anything I could do to prepare.

The wedding was on a Saturday at the end of August. The forecast called for rain; I remember fixating on the weather all week, fretting over the possibility. We had arranged to be married at an old farmhouse, outside in the gazebo. The morning came, cloudy and gray, but there was a window between showers at our scheduled time.

And I remember everything. The old mirror in the upstairs room I got ready in, the flowers, walking down the path to the gazebo flanked by my sisters, exchanging vows, the kiss, walking back down the aisle newly wedded, the reception afterward. At one moment, I stole away and slipped back upstairs for a few minutes. I sat at the dressing table in quiet reflection and just let myself feel. I was fully present.

I sent a text to my therapist and let her know that I had remained present the whole day. Her reply to me celebrated how momentous this event was.

Being able to remain present is still one of the greatest triumphs of my recovery. It's so funny, actually. I had always thought the most challenging things in my life would be achieving some really difficult career goal, or dealing with some challenging relationship. Turns out, it's the little, simple, quiet experience of being present.

The Human Drive

All humans are wired to experience several basic drives. Some drives are well-known: we have a drive for food, water, sleep, and sex. If we go too long without any of these, a tension builds in our bodies, calling our attention to it, until we satisfy the need. We call these tensions different things: hunger, thirst, sleepiness, etc. Most of these drives are primal, meaning they go way back in our evolutionary history. The drive to seek out sources of energy was necessary for life, and probably appeared shortly after life evolved. This drive shows up in our present lives in such things as a love for food, and an increasingly loud pang of hunger if we don't get some sustenance every few hours.

As I've said, most of these drives exist in most living things. But as we advanced in our evolution, we developed more, higher drives. And humans, being the most complex of all evolved species, developed lots of them. Psychologists identify them differently; some note, for example, a drive to defend, or a drive to achieve.

One thing I've come to understand as I worked with clients over the years is that the drives that set humans apart from all other species are our drives to connect and to make meaning. As humans, we have a *biological* drive to form connections with other people and to make meaning of our experiences and the world around us. These are survival drives, hardwired into us as fundamentally as the drives for thirst, food, safety, and sex. There were reasons for this; for example, we evolved to be social creatures, because very few of us can survive on our own. We need the support of other humans to survive, so evolving the drive to connect facilitated our species' survival.

While these drives were developing, evolution also gave us big brains. For some time, researchers have been trying to figure out exactly what facilitated the development of our big brains. Of course having bigger brains makes sense now, as our species came to dominate the world. But in the beginning, it was very costly and didn't make much sense. Biologically, brains are expensive.

First, they consume a lot of energy—by some estimates, 20 percent of all the energy our bodies use in terms of oxygen and blood flow. That's an awful lot for an organ that only accounts for 2 percent of our body's mass. We stole some of this energy by evolving weaker bodies, making us more susceptible to prey. But this didn't cover the difference, and we still needed to consume more calories, which meant we must spend more time finding food. That doesn't matter as much in modern society, but thousands of years ago, hunting and foraging required significantly more work and resources. And the gamble of bigger brains didn't pay off for hundreds of thousands of years. For a *long* time, bigger brains didn't make logical sense.

Bigger brains also require bigger heads, which make being born a more difficult and dangerous process. Women's bodies had to evolve a pelvic opening large enough for infants' brains to squeeze through. Still, this opening has a size limit, requiring that we're born in a very immature state when our brains are far from fully formed.

As a result, human babies are much more vulnerable than babies from other species. Most animals can walk within minutes of birth and are pretty independent within a year. Human babies, in contrast, require years of extended rearing and protection. This is partially where our drive to connect comes from. By evolving a need to connect to our young—and to connect with others who can help us with this extended period of rearing—we came to outlive those around us.

But many species evolved to be social without big brains—showing that this anatomy is not essential for this purpose. Tons of insect species form complex social structures and cooperate on a large scale with brains the size of a sesame seed, for example. So there must be additional reasons for our big brains.

Current thinking points to the need to distill lots of information in order to react to vastly different environments, as climates changed and humans migrated all over the world. As we grew bigger brains, we used this processing power to be more creative and adapt to different environments better than other creatures. These diverse challenges required us to make conclusions and then decisions based on them. So in short, we developed a drive to make meaning.

I take these two drives, to connect and to make meaning, very seriously in my work. Because these are hardwired drives, when we're unsuccessful in connecting or making meaning, this creates a lot of internal distress and anguish in our psyches, just like a lack of food creates anguish in our bodies. We literally thirst for connection. We hunger for meaning. Our brains create distress within us when we're not answering this drive in an attempt to call our attention to it, just as we grow hangry when we've not eaten.

The problem is that we haven't learned to recognize when this is happening. We try to respond to this tension in misguided ways: we connect in a fake way on social media, or we start to use substances to take away the feelings of emptiness.

It's long been known that helping people find healthy connections is key to most recovery programs. It's not just a nice add-on; it is fundamental to success. I also work with students to help their clients make meaning. I teach them there are millions of ways to make meaning of the world, but everyone must have at least one. Some people do this through a faith belief system; others make meaning through utilizing the scientific method. Some people look at the world through a more concrete lens; others are more metaphysical. Some people make meaning through their relationships with others; some people make meaning through their work. It doesn't seem to matter what way you make meaning, as long as it works for you.

The most well-known example of this comes from Viktor Frankl, who wrote *Man's Search for Meaning*. Dr. Frankl was a Jewish psychiatrist who was imprisoned in the German concentration camps during World War II. Here, he noticed that those prisoners in concentration camps who survived were those who were able to make meaning out of their existence. He went on to feature this as a core of his practice, using a new theory called logotherapy, after the Greek word for meaning (*logos*).

I have found a similar phenomenon in people recovering from substance use disorders. While there is no comparison between what happened in the concentration camps and the lives that people live at the worst of their addictions, those people who are able to come out the other side and find some meaning in what they went through are those who truly recover. Often, the meaning they make is to share their story—to connect with others on the path behind them to instill hope for further travel.

I believe this is fundamentally why 12-step recovery programs work: they meet the human drives to connect and make meaning. When people go to meetings, they are joining and connecting with others, forming authentic, supportive relationships. When they get a sponsor, they develop a special connection with one person. And by working the steps, they take the tangled web of their life and start to make meaning out of it. Part of step work includes uncovering what was causing you to behave in ways that didn't make sense (thereby making meaning), and to make amends to people you have hurt (thereby reconnecting). Once someone has progressed through the steps and is living a daily program, they continue to do service to others, deepening both meaning and connection.

But 12-step recovery doesn't work for everyone. It has a lot of problems. One unfortunate side effect of its success for some people is the belief that it is the panacea for everyone. Many treatment programs have a strong bias for imposing 12 step recovery on all their clients. In my mind, this is well-meaning, but unethical and potentially harmful. It is true that it is a powerful solution for some people with substance use disorders, but there are many more who don't see themselves reflected in the program. As a counselor, I think we need to strip back to why the program works for some people, and build a different solution for those whom it doesn't. I always take it back to the connection and meaning themes. For this client in front of me, what would provide healthy connection in their life? I've seen a person recover because they felt a deep connection to animals; becoming a vet tech provided a scaffold for feeling connection and was their path. I've seen a client develop healthy social lives that did not revolve around substance use, and feeling this connection and support was what worked for them.

The truth is, it is very egotistical and self-centered for me to think I know best what will work for any client. I am often wrong, and situating my counseling practice within this knowledge is fundamental to success. My job is to help clients craft a solution for themselves where *they* feel connected and a sense of meaning.

Wounded 12

Shame Spiral

Part of what fueled my return to use once I had landed in my position as a professor was the considerable shame I felt over losing my job as a mental health counselor. For legal and ethical reasons, I'd needed to be removed suddenly, with no notice or explanation given to any of my coworkers or my clients. I was simply . . . gone. This emptiness and lack of closure haunted me. Coworkers were sent a brief email saying I was no longer working there. Clients received a similar letter or phone call, with a referral to another therapist.

The ending of a relationship between a therapist and a client has a special term in our literature: termination. Termination is considered a vital part of the therapeutic process, as most clients have not experienced many good endings in their lives. We are trained to guide them through the process of the ending of our time together—providing time for reflection, gratitude, or sorrow, and saying goodbye.

Due to the unique features of a therapeutic relationship, a goodbye is usually really a goodbye. In American culture, we are averse to saying good-bye. We let relationships trail off, with platitudes like "We'll keep in touch," or "Let's do lunch sometime." We don't address the loss; instead, we just divert our attention to new things. But therapists don't get to say, "We'll keep in touch," or "Let's do lunch sometime." Ethics requires us to maintain professionalism, no matter how close we get to our clients, and this requires having a clean and clear ending when the client has met their goals.

Termination, when done right, can be incredibly healing for clients. They get to have a good ending in their life, and they can transfer this learning to other relationships.

I've learned that termination is not just a necessary step for clients; it is necessary for the therapist as well. We get invested in our clients' lives, sometimes working with clients for many years, and going through the termination process allows for closure for us as well.

Because of my use, I did damage to my clients, because I did not allow them to go through this process. And I did damage to myself, because I didn't get to go through it either. In a real professional and ethical sense, I abandoned my clients. This fact bore a hole deep into my soul, set up shop, and festered.

As I've shared, it's amazing what shame can do to a person. Some people might look at my transition to teaching as a blessing, a gift of the universe to catch me as I was falling. That's not how I saw it. I merely saw myself as *banished*: banished from the land of clinical practice, not good enough to see clients. I went to work every day with this belief.

As I passed the two-year mark of fake sobriety, l began to look for clinical psychologist positions. At two years, the state would allow me to see clients again. Every couple of weeks, I would apply for a position. I wasn't picky. It's amazing how motivating shame can be, in its own funny way. It caused me to think, *Any clinical position that will get me back in the game will do.*

A couple of months into my search, I happened upon a job listing for a small private practice in Minneapolis that was looking for a third psychologist. When I submitted my materials, I was contacted immediately. The couple who ran the practice were impressed with my credentials and training, and after a quick interview, I was offered the position.

The position was wrong for me in so many ways, but that didn't matter to me. I needed to find a way to leave the school, to prove that I was good enough to see clients. And when I got the job, I only felt more anxious. *This has to work*, I told myself.

I arranged with my school to have a transition semester that spring, wherein I would work part-time for the school as I built up my client caseload. It often takes several months for a new clinician to build up a full-time schedule and pay, and I needed the steady income the school could provide to bridge this gap.

When I started the new counseling job that March, it became pretty clear early on that I was an awful fit for the job. The clients the clinic specialized in, and the type of services they focused on, were not an ideal match for my training and experience. The anxious urgency I felt about wanting the job quickly turned into the daily dread of being there. I floundered mightily for a few weeks, and it became evident that I wasn't going to last. The day I made the decision to leave, about a month in, was the day the owners had decided to fire me. I agreed to work another few weeks, to transition the clients I did have to other providers. Then I scampered quickly back to the school and asked if it were possible for me to return full-time to teaching there. They obliged.

I had failed in my attempt to outrun shame, and failed miserably. I hadn't successfully returned from the banished land and proven my worth. Instead, I had proven my belief that I wasn't good enough. In my attempt to clear some land by starting a controlled fire, I had set off an inferno that had destroyed the whole forest. The shame muck that I had been wading in since I arrived at the school became a stormy sea of shame that threatened to engulf me. I went into a deep depression, and my thoughts of wanting to die returned.

In the middle of all this, I reached the three-year mark of my monitoring program, which meant I was eligible for graduation from the monthly requirements of drug tests, reports, and case management. Because I had never had a positive urine test, and because all my reports were good, the monitoring agency agreed to release me.

Looking back, I can see I had many opportunities to be honest about my use and my struggles. The system was in place to provide me with help. But once again, my shame was so deep over what had happened about my job, my soul could not bear the additional shame of admitting failure at recovery.

All of this was the perfect fuel for a relapse. Indeed, I had been planning my relapse on opioids at this point for months. With the timing of the urine screens, I knew I couldn't get away with using any opiates during my monitoring. But for about a year, every now and then, an opportunity would arise for me to steal a Vicodin or Percocet from a friend or family member. And so I had amassed a collection of five pills, which I squirreled away in the corner of my underwear drawer. About once a week or so, I would sink my hand down to the bottom of the drawer and fondle the collection, just to confirm they were still there. I found it oddly comforting to do so.

And then the day came that April when I got my release date from monitoring. I had my final meeting with my case worker. On the last day, my color happened to be called requiring one final urine test. I left work a few minutes early to go to the testing site. I had a conversation with another participant in the waiting room who was just starting her monitoring. I shared that this was my last day. She told me congratulations.

Then I drove straight home, walked directly back to the bedroom, pulled out all five pills, and took them at once.

Healing 21

The Orchid Hypothesis

I deliver one of the patient lectures at Hazelden Betty Ford once a month. Patients go to two 30-minute lectures a day, receiving education on various recovery topics, from healthy communication to relapse prevention. Many of the lectures are focused on concepts of 12-Step recovery. The one I give combines a number of topics. It is a conglomeration of things I've learned over the past two decades—including a little psychology, a little biology, and a little 12-step recovery. It even includes a little history.

I begin by outlining how addicts can live in one of two states: one where they are active in their addiction, and one where they are active in their recovery. Each state is characterized by how the person views and interacts with the world. These states are most easily organized as different views of the past, the present, and the future. I illustrate these differences in a table.

	Addiction	Recovery
Past	Anger	Acceptance
Present	**D**ishonesty	**H**onesty
	Insecurity	**O**penness
	Conditionality	**W**illingness
Future	Fear	Trust; Faith

I begin in the upper left-hand corner. People, when they are active in their addiction, tend to look at the past through the lens of anger. The world has not been fair to them. People have mistreated them. They are not where they are "supposed" to be. They are full of resentments—at other people, and at the world in general. They will also turn this anger inward and experience self-hatred.

Popping down to the bottom of this column, I explain how people, when they are active in their addiction, tend to look at the future through the lens of fear. They don't know what's going to happen, but they're pretty sure it's not going to be good. They feel they must remain on alert at all times, prepared for all the bad stuff ahead. They will read the worst intent in any person or situation. They are perpetual pessimists, always finding the worst in any possibility.

Now, what's really interesting about these two emotions, anger and fear, is that they are *activating* emotions. They spur a physical response in our bodies. They do this through the autonomic nervous system. This part of the nervous system operates unconsciously. We don't have to think to make anything happen; our bodies respond automatically. The part of the autonomic nervous system that gets activated by anger and fear is called the sympathetic nervous system. Most people know this as the fight-or-flight response. It's activated primarily through the release of the neurotransmitters epinephrine and norepinephrine.

When the sympathetic nervous system gets activated, a whole host of biological changes cascade through our body. Our blood vessels constrict, and our blood pressure goes up. Our bodies divert energy from the periphery to our major muscle groups. Our breathing quickens, delivering more oxygen to our muscles. All of this is to help our bodies fight off an attacker, or flee the situation. Other things happen as well. Our pupils constrict, giving us better vision on the horizon, where danger might lie. Our digestion even stops. Our bodies are doing a quick calculation: it takes energy to digest food; does our body want to use that energy that way, or divert it toward keeping us safe? So it shuts down digestion temporarily to aid in the fight-or-flight response.

Now there are lots of things that can activate the sympathetic nervous system, but constantly feeling anger and fear are two of them. It's important to know that the sympathetic nervous system has a complementary part, called the parasympathetic nervous system. It does the exact *opposite* as the sympathetic nervous system. It acts primarily through the neurotransmitter acetylcholine. It slows our breathing, opens up our blood vessels, and cues things like digestion to resume. In a healthy nervous system, the two parts act in concert with one another: danger presents itself, our sympathetic nervous system activates, we get out of danger, and our parasympathetic nervous system kicks in and brings our bodies back to a state of safety and rest.

Up and down, but all within a normal range. At least, that's how it's designed to act. The problem is our bodies haven't evolved to tell the difference between a saber-tooth-tiger-is-chasing-me kind of stress, and I-might-lose-my-job kind of stress; our bodies react exactly the same way. So our sympathetic nervous system starts going outside of the normal limits, resulting in spikes and crashes of hormones, called hyperarousal and hypoarousal. Our bodies are no longer operating in the normal nervous system rhythm with the parasympathetic nervous system.

At this point, it's important to know that norepinephrine and epinephrine are short-term hormones and neurotransmitters; our bodies can't produce them in large numbers for long. When our stress is constantly elevated, our bodies begin to release a different substance, cortisol, which is a stress hormone. And long-term release of cortisol leads to the development of a number of chronic health conditions. This is because cortisol does things like raise our blood glucose and suppress the immune system, digestion, and reproduction. We also have mental health conditions that develop. So when our systems get stuck in high gear, we develop things like heart disease, chronic pain, anxiety, digestive problems, sleep problems, restlessness, sexual dysfunction, weight gain, and hostility/rage. When our system gets stuck in low gear, a different constellation of long-term health conditions develops, things like depression, lethargy, exhaustion, chronic fatigue, dissociation, and again, poor digestion. Really, all kinds of chronic inflammation diseases develop. Because of this, most people with substance use disorders have a number of other physical and mental health conditions when they come into treatment.

So, what does this mean for recovery? Well, to be active in recovery means to shift how we look at the past, the present, and the future. When we're active in our addiction, we look at the past through the lens of anger. To be active in our recovery, we must view the past through the lens of acceptance. Now, mind you, acceptance doesn't mean approval; we don't have to *like* what's happened to us, but we can still stop judging it as wrong or unjust. We acknowledge the reality of the past, and stop fighting with its existence.

My favorite definition of acceptance, which I've talked about at other points in this book, is: letting go of *any* desire that the situation, person, or thing be any different than it is. We have no negative judgment of the situation, person, or thing; it simply exists. This allows us to move forward.

When we're active in our addiction, we look at the future through the lens of fear. To be active in our recovery, we must shift this lens to one of trust and faith—believing if we show up and represent ourselves as honestly as possible, things will work out.

I'm reminded here of the work of Dr. Angeles Arrien, a cultural anthropologist who studied indigenous wisdom traditions all over the world. She found that most cultures have four instructions for living fully. She distilled her findings it her book "The Four-Fold Way: Walking the Paths of the Warrior, Teacher, Healer, and Visionary." We are all expected to:

1. *Show up*. We must be present in our lives.
2. *Pay attention*. To what has heart and meaning. To what our needs are. To what the needs of others are.
3. *Be honest*. Without blame or judgment. Do what we say and say what we do. No need to manipulate to get a certain outcome.
4. *Let go of the outcome*. Practice acceptance in all of life. Have faith that everything will unfold as it needs to.

And here's the funny thing. We are now discovering that people who practice acceptance, and who live with trust and faith, actually *activate* their parasympathetic nervous system. Their bodies stop producing the stress hormones and start producing acetylcholine. In activating our parasympathetic nervous systems, our immune systems, digestive systems, and reproductive systems start coming back online. In activating our parasympathetic response, we bring our nervous systems back into a healthy rhythm. Our bodies begin to change, calming down that whole host of long-term health conditions.

So that leaves us with the present. Anyone who's been active in 12-step recovery will easily tell you they're instructed to live using the acronym HOW, which stands for Honest, Open, and Willing.

- We are supposed to be *honest* in our communication, with ourselves and with others. We don't lie.
- We are supposed to be *open*—open to the idea that our best thinking got us in a pretty crappy place, and that maybe, just maybe, there are different ways of getting through life.
- And we are supposed to be *willing*—willing to try the suggestions of people who are trying to help us.

And that got me thinking one day. How do we live in the present moment when we're active in addiction? I came up with the acronym DIC, standing for Dishonest, Insecure, and Conditional.

- We're *dishonest*. We're constantly withholding information or manip- ulating to get something we want. We're always working some angle.
- We're *insecure*. We're perpetually unsure of ourselves and our place in this world.
- And we are *conditional*. We're forever saying, "I'll do this, if this happens...." "I'll go here, when that happens...."

Sometimes it's hard to know what lens I'm using to look at the past or the future, but I've learned I can always check in on the present moment. And one day it hit me that I can do this by asking myself the question: *"HOW* am I doing? Am I being a *DIC?"* How Honest, Open, and Willing (HOW) am I being *in this moment?* Versus, am I being Dishonest, Insecure, or Conditional (DIC) anywhere in my life? Stopping and asking myself this humorous question can immediately let me know if I'm being active in my addiction, or active in my recovery. And if I am being dishonest, insecure, or conditional in some way, it gives me the pathway back to being active in recovery: getting honest, using my resources to determine a good way to react, and be willing to put those plans and ideas into action.

All of this is important for most people, but it may be even more critical for people with substance use disorders. Here, I like to tell the story of orchids and dandelions.

Several decades ago, researchers started asking the question: *why do we still have depression in our species?* They wondered why, if it wasn't helpful in some way, it hadn't yet evolved out of our species. And they started to pull at the threads of this question.

Over time, they discovered there did seem to be a genetic predisposition for a number of mental health conditions—including depression, anxiety, and yes, substance use disorders—in that the more of a certain cluster of genes you had, the more likely you were to have mental health problems in life. But they also found this very peculiar group of people who had all the same genetic markers, but seemed to be thriving in life. They were successful, happy, and even prosperous.

And then it hit them: these genes don't code for things like depression and anxiety and substance use disorders. What they code for is actually *sensitivity to the environment.* So that when the environment is not supportive, these people are more deeply affected, and therefore respond more intensely. This is why they develop depression. This is why they become anxious. This is why they drink, or use, or try to escape. They are more miserable than most people.

But the opposite is also true: that when the environment is supportive, these people are more sensitive to this as well, and therefore also respond more intensely in this direction. But this time, the response is joy and creativity and engagement, and usually success.

And researchers began to use the analogy of orchids and dandelions. Most people, they said, are relatively hardy, like dandelions. Dandelions are resilient; they can grow most anywhere—in a crack in a sidewalk, on a lawn, or in a greenhouse. And they are relatively *insensitive* to the environment; they respond the same way in each place and look pretty much the same no matter where they are.

But some of us . . . some of us are like orchids. You can't plant us in a crack in a sidewalk; we will wither and die. But if you put us in the right environment—the right greenhouse, with the right soil, and light, and water, we will bloom magnificently. We are more sensitive to the environment and respond accordingly.

Now, we shouldn't knock dandelions. Most of the world is dandelions. We need dandelions. Hell, my wife is a dandelion. She can go through an experience that would break down most people and be pretty much okay. She worked in a job that she hated for years. Couldn't really stand it. But it didn't seem to get her too down. She'd just get up every day and go back in. She was not very sensitive to the stress in her environment.

Me, I had a job I hated, and I lasted all of two months. By the end of it, my hair started to fall out; I lost my appetite and couldn't eat. I became deeply anxious. I was more *sensitive* to the environment, and my body responded to this. And now that I have a job that fits me well, I'm thriving. I'm extremely happy. I can access my creativity and find new and inventive ways of teaching and communicating. I can write a book like this one.

As it turns out, our species evolved to have both kinds of people: dandelions and orchids. Having both actually benefits our species. We have a hardy stock of dandelions that form the bulk of our species, and keeps us going. And a certain percentage of our species have these special orchid genes that allow them to push the edges of who we—as a species—are and what we can do. These are the people who explore and discover new lands and knowledge. These are the people who create and invent and repair. The downside is that these people are also susceptible to things like depression and anxiety and substance use disorders. So researchers now understand the answer to their original question: this is why we still have depression in our species. It's the trade-off for innovation.

But back to why the orchid hypothesis is important for people with substance use disorders to know and understand. If we go back and look at that original chart that outlined the lenses through which we look at the past, present, and future, we can apply the orchid hypothesis. If we understand that most people with addiction have this cluster of genes, then we can understand that they are more sensitive to the environment. So, people with substance use disorders are more *sensitive* to the left side of the chart; constant feelings of anger, and fear, and insecurity are thereby more likely to release the stress hormones and neurotransmitters, and therefore activate the sympathetic nervous system. These "orchids" are more likely to get their nervous system rhythms out of whack, and therefore develop all of those health conditions. Living on this side of the chart is, in effect, like living in a crack in a sidewalk.

But we must keep in mind that the opposite is also true: people with substance use disorders are also more *sensitive* to the effects of living on the right side of the chart. These are people, whose bodies, when they regularly practice acceptance, and openness, and trust and faith, are *more likely* to release the neurotransmitter acetylcholine, thereby activating their parasympathetic nervous system. And regular activation of this part of the autonomic nervous system brings the whole nervous system back into a healthy rhythm and calms down all of those long-term health conditions. But something additional happens. Because this is akin to living in a greenhouse, these are people who come to thrive.

There's a phrase that's used to describe people in active 12 Step recovery: happy, joyous, and free. We are also given the Promises, which outline a life of serenity, balance, and meaningful service and connection. All of this happens because we are more *sensitive* to the effects of acceptance, openness, and faith.

This is the paradox of addiction. We have a set of genes that make us more susceptible to the most miserable lives, but we also have the set of genes that makes us more susceptible to the best possible lives. But it means we must be very intentional about how we live. We must ensure that our environments are supportive, that they allow us to practice that honesty, trust, and faith. We have to pay attention to where we live, who we are in relationships with, and how we spend our days. We have to make our own greenhouses.

Acceptance, honesty, trust, and faith are core principles of 12-step recovery. People who practice the steps, particularly steps one, two, and three, engage in a daily focus on these principles. But I also must fervently point out that 12-step recovery is not the only way to achieve these results. Anyone who can find a way to elicit these principles in their lives will get this result. And there are many ways to do this. There are cognitive behavioral therapies designed around these principles. Many religions, particularly Buddhism, are centered around the daily practice of these principles. Many cultures, throughout history and around the world have figured out these concepts, without knowing the biology behind them. This wisdom has been available to us for millennia. We're just discovering how to describe it using the language of science and biology.

Wounded 13

AA World Convention

About a year after I came back to the graduate school full time, I was asked to represent the school at the World Convention for Alcoholics Anonymous, which was taking place in Atlanta over the July fourth holiday. It is the largest gathering of people in 12-step recovery in the world, and it only happens once every five years. There's space for sponsors and vendors to spread their word or hock their fares. Sixty thousand AA members from all over the world were coming to this three-day event, to, as AAers put it, "share their experience, strength, and hope" with one another. For me, it was a three-day business trip to staff Hazelden Betty Ford's booth, spreading the word about our services and products.

Sarah and I had moved in together the month before. We moved across the hall from my small one-bedroom apartment to a three-bedroom apartment that would have room for both of us. My leases allowed an overlap of two weeks, so I could take my time moving my stuff over and then have ample time to clean.

This wasn't long after I had relapsed on pills the evening I came off my monitoring program, and I wanted to make the most of it. *If I was going to relapse, let's do it right*, I thought. My plan started innocently enough. I decided alcohol was the best substance to use. I had never really had any issues with drinking. It was never my preferred substance, but it would allow me to get loose for a few hours, and then be presentable to others by night. So I decided that on that Friday, I would spend a couple of hours moving and cleaning. As a reward, I would go buy a pint of vodka for use only in the old apartment. My rule was: whatever I didn't drink that day, I'd have to throw out. I vowed never to allow alcohol in the new apartment.

At 8 a.m. when Sarah left for work, I drove to the liquor store and bought a pint. I drank a few shots worth, poured the rest out, and disposed of the bottle before Sarah got home that evening. It went so well that I decided that I would repeat the experience. But the following week, it seemed like such a waste to throw out the liquor, so I told myself that I would allow myself to hide the bottle in the old kitchen. But I would limit my drinking only to the old apartment. I would not bring it into the new one, and I would stop once the lease ended. *I just need the time to say goodbye, that's all*, I rationalized.

My lease on the old apartment ended after two weeks. My drinking did not.

Each week, the rules changed, becoming more fluid. *I will now hide the pints in my office desk in the new apartment, but I will still only buy pints.* The next week, I decided, *Buying pints isn't cost effective; I should just buy a fifth, but I will absolutely only hide it in my belongings.* But I really enjoyed cold vodka, so the next week I decided my hiding spot would be in the vegetable bin in the refrigerator, which was opaque and never used. And then I got tired of vodka and soda, so I started buying mixed margaritas. I had a rule to only drink on Fridays during the day, when Sarah was at work. Soon I expanded that to include Wednesday evenings, when Sarah was playing softball. I was usually in bed by the time she returned, so I could get away with it.

It was always about what I could get away with.

Soon, I was drinking most days if I had any time alone in the apartment. Within weeks, my drinking had spread to evenings even when Sarah was at home. I would open a can of soda, drink a few swallows, and replace that with a shot or two of vodka. I had broken every single rule I had made.

So, when I was asked to travel to the AA convention in Atlanta, I jumped at the chance. Getting to travel alone and sleep by myself in a secluded hotel room, it would be an opportunity for me to drink every day, without worrying about Sarah detecting it. Of course there wouldn't be alcohol at any of the convention events—it was a dry event. But I'd have plenty of time alone.

I started drinking at the airport bar on the way out. I got a vodka and coke, so if by chance I ran into anyone who knew me, I could tell them I was just having a soda while waiting for my flight.

I had planned for the trip like only an addict could. I mapped the closest hotels to the event, and then looked at where the nearest liquor stores were. Superimposed on all of this was the public transportation network that would facilitate my travel between all three places. I was able to locate a MARTA stop a few blocks from a liquor store downtown. After landing at the airport, once I bought my alcohol, I rolled my luggage the half mile to the hotel.

For the next three days, I drank each evening, alone, in my hotel room. I reveled at the idea that I could leave the bottle out, without worrying about it being seen. I staffed the Hazelden Betty Ford booth all day and talked to hundreds of people in recovery about all the good work my organization was doing.

Funny enough, I was wearing a T-shirt with the name of our graduate school on it: Hazelden Graduate School of Addiction Studies. Many people found the shirt quite humorous, believing that it was a joke.

"I got a graduate degree in drinking too," they'd laugh and say.

"No, really, we're a real school; we train addiction counselors," I'd have to tell them.

People who come to an AA World Convention are serious about recovery. They have paid thousands of dollars to travel, sometimes across the world, to be immersed in as deeply committed a group of people as there is. They are eager to share stories of how AA changed their lives, how destitute they had been, and how much they are flourishing now. Most of them knew the Hazelden Betty Ford name, as we published many supportive materials for recovery.

During the day, I spent hours listening to story after story of lives turning around, of how ecstatic people were to meet sober people from all over the US and world, of just how happy and giddy they were. I received many thanks for our materials and treatment centers.

I always smiled politely and received the thanks. I offered congratulations when people told me how many years they had been in recovery. But inside, I was just counting down the time to when I could return to the hotel room and open that bottle.

Each night, I grabbed dinner on the way to the room, opened the door, and poured myself the first drink. I felt a freedom, knowing no one I knew could walk in and discover me. When I was at home, I always dealt with the off chance that Sarah could get off work early or come home for some other reason. I was always on guard. When I took out a bottle to pour a drink, I was always hyperaware, listening for the front door to unlock. Anytime a bottle was out of a drawer, I always had a plan front of mind of how to hide it quickly were something to happen. But not here. Here, I was free.

For most people, the AA World Convention is a time to connect, a time to experience the bliss of recovery with thousands of other people. For me, the bliss came from dancing alone around my hotel room, swinging the vodka bottle around and taking deep swallows. I could spill without being paranoid that the smell left in the carpet would reveal me. This was my glee. I would feel the warm wave of alcohol move through my body and sway to its influence. One of the effects of having had gastric bypass surgery is that it doesn't take as much alcohol to feel drunk, so I usually didn't need more than a few drinks. I drank until I started to feel a headache. Then I crawled into bed and drifted off to sleep. The next day, I would again listen to people expound on the rewards of recovery. With each story, the voice inside of me that said I was miserable grew a little louder.

There was one difference, though, this summer with my use. I was no longer alone with my secret. While I was under the monitoring program, it wasn't possible for me to talk to anyone about my use. Part of monitoring involved quarterly reports from my sponsor, therapist, psychiatrist, and boss to my case manager. If I told any of them I had been using, they would have to report it. Therefore, if I told one person, everyone would know. It really was all or nothing. I wasn't ready for all, so I chose nothing.

Therefore, for years in therapy, I never talked about how I struggled with still using. I focused on interpersonal or work issues with a variety of therapists. One time, I decided to test my therapist at the time by admitting that I had been taking a lot of ibuprofen and acetaminophen, and that it felt compulsive. She told me she would have to report it, and did. So I knew there was no safety in talking about the truth.

I was with a different therapist now, doing some trauma work. The first session I had with her after I came off of monitoring, I walked in, and revoked all my releases of information, meaning that she could not tell anyone else what I was about to tell her. Then I told her everything. For the first time in three years, I was no longer alone. I wasn't ready for that information to go beyond that office, but finally I wasn't alone.

Healing 22

The Cosmological Constant

Albert Einstein is arguably the most famous scientist of all time. His genius is universally admired. His rise to fame is well documented. Unable to find employment at a university, which was his greatest desire, he accepted a job as a lowly patent clerk in Bern, Switzerland. As the job did not occupy much of his mental energy, he spent a great deal of his time conducting thought experiments and writing up the results for publication. The turning point in his career came in 1905, commonly called his "miracle year," when he published four academic papers, each revolutionizing the field of physics. This included a theory of special relativity, which explained how speed affects mass, time, and space. His papers were, to everyone, mind-blowing and field-revolutionizing. From there, Einstein built a reputation as a leading theorist and spent the rest of his life in academia.

About a decade after his miracle year, Einstein was working on a theory of general relativity, where he sought to explain gravity. He generated a set of equations seeking to explain gravity in terms of space-time. In everything he was coming up with, his equations kept predicting that the universe was expanding. However, the assertion at the time from the scientific community was that the universe was static, neither contracting nor expanding. Influenced by this zeitgeist, Einstein created a variable to account for what his peers thought and added it to his equations. Called the *cosmological constant*, this variable zeroed out the expansion that his equations had predicted. He published his work this way.

However, ten years later, scientists confirmed through observations that the universe was indeed expanding. It turned out that Einstein had been right in his original equations, but he had become swayed by popular thought. He came to deeply regret not following the data that he had originally uncovered. It's been reported that Einstein called the cosmological constant his "biggest blunder."

I think about this cosmological constant a lot, especially when students or clients express difficulty understanding how people can react to situations in seemingly irrational ways. I tell them about Einstein's cosmological constant to illustrate how powerful the pull can be to deny what reality is telling us in favor of adopting the beliefs of those around us. When people are outraged that some people decline to get vaccines, citing a number of concerns, I point out that in these individual's circles, the prevailing wisdom is that the vaccine is harmful, not necessary, or the subject of a government conspiracy. It is true that a few people have reactions to vaccines, but the net improvement to the individual and society is well documented. Clearly all the scientific data support vaccines' safety and effectiveness, but none of this matters to these people. Einstein had all the data in front of him, yet he bowed to social pressure to conform his equations to current theory. If even the smartest person of the last century is subject to this influence, how can we be surprised that others are too?

The cosmological constant shows up in a lot of my work. Most seemingly rational people usually hold lots of irrational beliefs—meaning even when all the data show something not to be true, they hold firm to their belief. Hundreds of psychological studies show the human drive to do this. In fact, we seem to be programmed to do this. As our species evolved, our greatest strength was our ability to cooperate. This meant reaching group consensus was important, and therefore evolution selected for it. We needed to trust the conclusions of others and act in concert with them. For example, tribe members may have had different ideas about the best way to collectively hunt, but one idea had to be agreed upon and carried out. So the cosmological constant is actually a holdover from evolution. Now our species dominates the world, and the scientific method is used to advance us. But this cosmological constant holdover remains.

I also realize that I am not immune to this tendency. I often think about the cosmological constant in my daily life. When I'm feeling a pull to do something or be a certain way as a result of influence from people around me that contradicts what I know, I try to ask myself, *Am I doing a cosmological constant here? Am I succumbing to the social pressure? If I strip away the social pull I'm feeling, what does the data tell me?* Asking these questions allows me to gain awareness of the invisible force of social pressure, bring it into my consciousness, label it, and then work through it. This process builds a pause into my response, allowing me to switch from a place of reaction to a place of action. Sometimes I still go with the social pressure, and that's okay—again, sometimes cooperation trumps individual knowledge, but this way, I do so with awareness of what I'm choosing.

A great example of how the cosmological constant shows up in my life involves my body and my appearance. We are bombarded daily by news stories, advertisements, and even doctors who assert that fat people are lazy, unhealthy, and unhappy. That we are fat because we lack willpower and self-control, and that losing weight universally leads to a better life, because all thin people are healthy. And the path to losing weight is dieting and exercise. I believed these myths for a long time. I did a lot of damage to my body because of these myths, some of which I outline in this book.

However, over the past decade, a lot of people have challenged these myths. When we look at the hard data, a different picture emerges. It turns out that every single one of these myths is wrong. Fat people aren't lazy; studies have shown they have only slightly lower activity levels than "normal" weight people. They're also not universally unhealthy—anywhere from one-third to two-thirds of people with higher weights show all other normal health markers including blood pressure, blood sugars, cholesterol, and strength. They're also not all unhappy, and the unhappiness that is experienced is more related to weight bias and stigma in society than to the actual experience of being heavier—showing that for most people the stigma associated with being overweight does more damage to a person's body than the weight itself. We've also definitively learned that willpower and self-control have very little to do with one's weight; higher weights are caused by a complicated confluence of genetic, behavioral, and societal factors. And the biggest myth of all might be that all thin people are inherently healthy; for example, it turns out a fit overweight person has a lower risk of developing diabetes than an unfit thin person. Finally, the path of diets definitely does not work; 95 percent of them fail, and 60 percent of people actually end up at a higher weight than when they started the diet because of how the body responds to being starved.

So in short, weight has a lot less to do with a person's health than is widely believed. Applying the cosmological constant, I constantly have to work to step back and look at the data, instead of the giving in to the incessant pull and chatter from the world around me. When I do this, I actually feel an affinity for what Einstein went through; I feel a strange closeness and understanding for his biggest blunder. That social pull is *strong*. But I also feel comforted by knowing that eventually, most of the time, the data prevail.

Healing 23

Paradoxical Life

A couple of years ago I became obsessed with paradoxes. A paradox is a phenomenon whereby two contradictory or opposing things are both true. For humans, this often creates a tension in the mind as one struggles to hold on to both truths simultaneously. Carl Jung, an important early psychiatrist, focused some of his work on paradoxes. He believed that humans are at their most "humanness" when they are able to hold two opposite truths at the same time. He called it "our most valuable spiritual possession." Brene Brown, too, highlights the paradoxes that are fundamental to the human experience.

That summer, I was starting to see all the paradoxes that existed around me. The first was the paradox that people are both powerless and powerful beyond all measure. A great deal of what happens in our lives is completely out of our control; at the same time, we can exert incredible influence on our and others' lives. Another paradox that came to me is that we are both incredibly fragile and incredibly resilient, both at the same time. We are capable of withstanding great stresses and challenges, while also being subject to a delicate existence that can change in an instant. Humans are also simultaneously capable of magnificent acts of goodwill and horrible acts of destruction. Both of these abilities exist in each of us at all times.

As I contemplated these paradoxes, I could feel the tension rise inside of me. My mind wanted to latch on to one side or the other; holding both truths in full view of the other required some effort. I forced myself to endure this discomfort, and over time, experienced a growing sense of calm while holding both sides simultaneously.

I also started to become aware of the paradoxes that exist in nature. The most famous one is the discovery that light is both a particle and a wave. For centuries, people had been trying to resolve the question of whether light was a wave or a particle. Various experiments came to contradictory conclusions; at times light behaved as a particle, and at times it behaved as a wave. Finally, scientists came to terms that light is both. Albert Einstein wrote about this elegantly in his book, *The Evolution of Physics*: "It seems as though we must use sometimes the one theory [wave theory] and sometimes the other [particle theory], while at times we may use either. We are faced with a new kind of difficulty. We have two contradictory pictures of reality; separately neither of them fully explains the phenomena of light, but together they do."

Indeed, there is evidence that all reality consists of oppositions existing together. Atoms are made up of protons, neutrons, and electrons. Protons carry a positive charge; electrons a negative charge. Only together do they constitute an element of matter. This holds true even at lower levels of matter. Protons and neutrons are constructed by combining up and down quarks, each with different positive and negative charges. On a larger scale, life itself is dependent on the presence of both chaos and order. Order provides the structure and organization needed for life, with components like amino acids, DNA, and cells. Chaos provides the randomness and flexibility necessary for natural selection and evolution to happen. Both are necessary. Life, it turns out, is rarely either/or, but rather both/and.

Twelve-step recovery also considers several paradoxes. In a famous story from the second edition of the *Big Book* called "The Professor and the Paradox," the author outlines four essential paradoxes of recovery:

- *We Surrender to Win.* It is the act of surrendering to our disease that makes winning recovery possible.
- *We Give Away to Keep.* Twelve-step recovery posits that the only way to keep our sobriety is to keep giving away what we've learned to others on the same path.
- *We Suffer to Get Well.* The only route to wellness requires a trip through suffering.
- *We Die to Live.* Finally, in order to live in recovery, we must allow our addict selves to die.

Beyond these paradoxes, addicts are called upon daily to move through life according to the principles of *acceptance* and *change*. These two actions are paradoxical; when we practice acceptance, we are working to accept things as they are while letting go of any desire to make them different. When we focus on change, inherent in this is refusing to accept the current circumstances. The Serenity Prayer, often used to open and close meetings, reminds us of this: "Grant me the serenity to accept the things I cannot change, the courage to change the things I can, and the wisdom to know the difference."

Humans have been contemplating the seemingly natural law of paradoxes for millennia. Ancient Chinese philosophy distilled this into the concept of yin-yang more than 2,500 years ago, represented by the well-known, black-and-white *taijitu* symbol. Yin-yang posits that all life is the balanced combination of opposites. Day and night, life and death, fire and water...not only does everything have an opposite, but its opposite is necessary to define the original. We cannot know that something has a bottom without also knowing it has a top. And it is the relationship of the top to the bottom that defines something. There is no shadow without light. Here, opposites are not seen as competing with one another, but rather complementing one another to create reality. This philosophy does not find tension in the opposites; instead, it encourages us to always be seeking balance.

Looking at my own life, I can see that my existence is often paradoxical. For years, I was an active addict, while at the same time serving as an expert helping others recover. I was both destroying myself while I helped others improve. Even today, I am both wounded and healing at the same time. And I always have been. I've come to believe that all of us are.

As I spent time contemplating paradoxes, I started to notice them in my clinical work. Often the distress my clients were feeling was directly related to experiencing a paradox. Clients talked in sessions about trying to figure out what feeling they were experiencing. Through conversation, we discovered that they were actually experienced a number of emotions, many of them contradictory.

One client expressed distress that she couldn't figure out if she was scared or angry at something in her life. I helped her consider the possibility that she was feeling both those things. Further, we discussed the possibility that it wasn't feeling scared or angry that was causing her distress, but rather her distress was being caused by her belief that she had to be experiencing on or the other. Only after we allowed both feelings to exist simultaneously was she able to move through them.

Another client brought in the question of whether or not she should stay in her marriage; over several sessions, we uncovered that she both wanted to stay and leave. I worked to help her get to a place where she could allow both truths to exist simultaneously. She had a belief that she needed either to 100 percent want to leave, or 100 percent want to stay. Only after we created a space where both desires could exist together was it possible for her to navigate a path that worked for her.

Since that time, I often find myself seeking out the paradox that is presenting itself, not only for clients, but for students and colleagues. I have begun shifting conversations away from trying to find a resolution, into creating space for the paradox to exist. I can say this has led me to an entirely different worldview. No longer do I feel a tension when a paradox arises; instead, I feel my body relax into it, knowing that I am seeing truth. Many times, until I've uncovered what the paradox is, I know I've not gotten to the core of the matter. I keep searching, and inevitably, it arises. Only then do I know I am seeing all parts of the issue. Now, instead of feeling tension, finding and experiencing the paradox brings about a sense of accomplishment.

Wounded 14

Ready

After I got honest with my therapist that spring, it took me another five months to be ready to tell the next person. Every week, I would go to therapy and talk about what I had been doing with my secret use. For weeks at a time, I would vacillate between wanting to stop and thinking that maybe I didn't really have a problem. I rarely drank more than three to four drinks after all, and usually only two to three times a week. For the average person, that would not classify as having a problem with alcohol. But I knew the criteria for a substance use disorder didn't focus heavily on the amount that person used, but rather on the lack of control over use and the resulting negative consequences.

I had plenty of those. And so my dance continued.

My mental health continued to slide. The depression that had deepened from my failed attempt to return to clinical work led to almost constant suicidal ideation. Every day, I would fantasize about a time when I could be dead and free from this life. It never progressed to the point of making a definite plan, but that didn't mean I wasn't in a great deal of pain. I would often ask Sarah to lay down on our bed with me, just to hold me and comfort me. I would have an intense urge to come clean to her during these times, to tell her everything, but a wall of sheer terror blocked that. As desperately as I wanted help, I was frozen by fear and shame.

And then, one day that September, it happened. I was able to vocalize to Sarah that there was something that I wanted her to know, but that I was scared to tell her. As we lay on the bed with her arms around me, I wept. The words were shouting in my head, but my tongue was frozen. And then Sarah said it. She asked if I had been using. The floodgates opened, and everything from the previous three years poured out of me. All the secrets, all the hiding, all the manipulation, all the lies that had existed for the entirety of our relationship. It must have been completely overwhelming for her to hear. But she listened. I talked for over an hour.

Once I had said everything, Sarah and I got up. She said she needed to go for a drive. (Whenever Sarah needed to take some space and process things, she always went for a drive.) She was gone for a couple of hours while I sat alone in the apartment, emotionally exhausted, unsure of what was going to happen next. Was Sarah going to leave me? Was I going to have to go back to treatment?

When she returned, she said I was going to have to tell my home group, my sponsor, and my psychiatrist. It was just as I had expected. The switch would need to flip open with everyone, all at once.

Over the next week, I recounted my hidden addiction over and over to the people in my life. Everyone was shocked, but supportive.

I used two last times in the next couple of weeks. About a week after I got honest with Sarah, I had to take one of my cats to the vet for a wound. I was sent home with antibiotics and four doses of a pain medication for the cat. Two blocks away from the vet, I pulled over and opened up the bag of medications. The pain medication was in liquid form. I was instructed to twist the top off the dispenser, and squirt the medication along my cat's gum line. *Don't do it*, I thought to myself as I took one of the vials out of the bag. *Stop, this is insane.* I twisted the top off and squirted the medication along my own gum line. I had just taken medicine prescribed for my cat. I did it, even knowing there was zero chance that I could feel any effects from this, given the difference in our sizes. I did it, even knowing that this meant my cat was going to suffer needlessly for me to try and get a fix.

This moment was my absolute bottom. I was completely, absolutely, and totally broken.

A few days later, I stole an Ambien from one of Sarah's family members during a visit to their house. That Sunday, I got up early and took it while Sarah was still in bed. I laid down on the couch in the living room as the sleepy, drowsy effects came over me. This was the last time I used.

That afternoon, I told Sarah about both uses. I notified the family member that I had stolen from them. And I called to schedule an assessment for my substance use. I was finally ready to quit.

There was something fundamentally different about this readiness. Prior to this, I never really *wanted* to stop using; I just knew I *needed* to. There was no real internal motivation to quit. I was afraid of losing my job, or my license, for sure, but I still wanted to use more than I wanted those things. What use did for me—how it numbed me and took me away from the painful experience of my emotions—was what I wanted more than anything else in the world. This had trumped everything.

Until now. For the first time in my life, I wanted something more than I wanted to use. On some deep unspoken level, I understood that if I continued to use, I would lose my relationship with Sarah. Being in a relationship with her and continuing to use could not both happen. And I wanted that relationship to continue more than I wanted to use. I could feel a fundamental internal shift. I had something to get sober for.

Looking back, I can see why this worked when nothing else had. I felt so little worth and regard for myself and my life, so I was not enough to get sober for. I cared so little for myself and didn't feel that I was deserving of a happy life. But I could recognize this relationship with Sarah was a good one. And I didn't want to lose it. She was worth it, even when I wasn't. Finally, I had found something to get sober for.

Sometimes when I describe this experience to others, they look at this negatively. Like this was the wrong way to get sober. That a person should want to do it for themselves, not for others. Counseling students are taught the difference between internal motivation and external motivation, and often external motivation is depicted as negative or wrong. Students will label a client as "externally motivated" as a judgment, meaning they are not really ready for recovery. I've come to believe that *every* person coming into recovery starts out with external motivation. It's the process of treatment and recovery to shift this motivation internally. Internal motivation comes over time, and it is what ultimately keeps a person sober, but people with substance use disorders must find something in their lives that they want more than they want to use before they can engage in recovery.

Going through this process myself changed how I counsel clients and teach students. In addiction counseling, we use a specific technique to help guide people through this process. It's called *motivational interviewing*, and it spends a lot of time helping clients resolve this fundamental conflict. Often students and counselors want to jump ahead in the treatment process, and start giving clients recovery treatment work without resolving this conflict.

But when the client hasn't identified a personal reason to get sober, they will always return to use, no matter how much treatment they've been given. Because of this, a huge amount of time and energy must be spent in resolving this conflict. This is not optional work; it is a necessary precursor to any treatment. It's the counselor's job to join the client in this conflict, not to convince them of any particular outcome, but to walk with them as they explore. We must also be ready to accept that this exploration might yield a decision that, in fact, no, there is nothing that the client wants more than to use. We must have fundamental acceptance of the client's conclusion in this case. We must respect that every person has the autonomy to make this choice.

It took me 13 years to resolve this conflict. But finally, I was ready.

Healing 24

To Be Alive Is to Change.

Change is hard for people. We resist it, even if the change can bring something good.

I used to spend a lot of time fantasizing about not having to change. I would wish that I could get something in my life to a certain place, and then have it not change. I did this with everything—my emotions, my career, my relationships. I wanted to achieve a certain level of recovery, and then freeze it in place. Even something as simple as getting my hair to a length I like; I would wish that it could just stay that way forever. It even bothered me that I had to clip my fingernails; wouldn't it be great if I could make them stay a certain length? In short, I elevated "steady" to an exalted position above "change."

I'm evolving my relationship to change in recovery. When confronted with a change, I say to myself, *You know, sometimes, every now and then, change brings good things.* When I benefit from a change, I spend some time noting this in my mind as evidence. I do this even with the little things.

Once, I was forced to try a different cat litter, because the one I'd used for years was out of stock. At first, I was annoyed, lamenting that I had to change something in my life. But wouldn't you know it, it turns out the alternate cat litter performed better. It became my preferred cat litter. I made a mental note of this to remind myself that change can bring good things.

Ultimately, change allows all healing to occur. If I cut my arm, it's not wounded forever; my immune system comes in and repairs the damage. Welcoming change is a critical component of all healing.

What I've come is to understand is that to be alive is to change. Life and change are synonymous. Scientists have been debating exactly how to define life for centuries. The current, most widely accepted definition is that life is a "self-sustaining chemical system that metabolizes and adapts to its environment." So, fundamentally, to be alive is to be constantly changing. Even at the cellular level, our cells are involved in constant change: letting molecules come and go through its borders, converting energy into work to power the cell, and having different proteins go around and clean up. Life doesn't exist without change. There is no such thing as *steady*. Steady means dead.

In many ways, making peace with life means accepting that things are constantly changing, and not fretting about this, but moving in concert with it. There is no such thing as getting to a certain point or outcome and then freezing. This is as impossible as breathing underwater.

But change is still hard.

Healing 25

Self-Care

Self-care is a common struggle for both students and clients. Okay, really, for everyone. I offer this chapter as a model for anyone to use; the examples are for counselors, but can be easily transferred.

My training program is dedicated to teaching students that self-care is vital for counseling work. We begin talking about it during orientation, and students get constant reminders of it every week. Counseling is hard work that involves an outpouring of energy; self-care is how we refuel our tanks. Without it, we burn out quickly. Self-care is not an optional part of this profession; indeed, it is the core of our power. If counselors are not taking care of themselves, they simply will not be available to do any counseling work with clients.

The biggest problem with teaching self-care is that it's such a large, nebulous subject. Most people don't really know what constitutes good self-care. Some people will say something about eating healthy and exercising, but self-care is about so much more than that.

I have found when educating students and clients alike, it's often necessary to teach self-care using a model. I've used different models of self-care over the years, but the one I've settled on is a bio-psycho-social-spiritual model.

Most counselors are familiar with the bio-psycho-social-spiritual model of *assessment*. When we conduct an assessment of any client, we're supposed to conduct a broad analysis of how this person is functioning and where their deficits or impairments may be.

I believe the same goes for counselors and self-care.

When I conduct an audit of my self-care practices, I ask myself a few questions about how I am meeting my biological, psychological, social, and spiritual needs. A quick internal scan can highlight issues. I teach my students and clients to do the same thing. Here is my guide, which includes some questions to ask.

Biological

- *Basically, how is my sleeping, eating, and pooping?*

In my experience, getting one's sleep regulated has the biggest return on investment of any self-care activity. Sleep is critical to healthy functioning. It must be; otherwise, evolution wouldn't have selected for it, given that being asleep puts us in such a vulnerable position. Memory consolidation, cell repair, immune system functioning—all of these are key functions of sleep. Each of us has different requirements for sleep, but most adults average needing seven to nine hours per night. When deficits exist, I ask students to commit to working on their sleep, using appropriate sleep hygiene when necessary. There are many guides online.

After sleep, it's important to pay attention to our nutritional needs. We can ask ourselves:

- *Am I eating food that helps my body function well?*
- *Am I taking regular breaks during the day to eat?*
- *Am I making sure my nutritional needs are being met?*

- *Am I getting enough protein, fat, and carbohydrates?*

Many counselors will skip meals or grab a bag of chips in between clients in order to get more work done. While we all have to do this occasionally, if it's happening with any frequency, I encourage people to address it.

Connected to our nutrition is our processing of food.

- *How is my digestive system working?*

Digestive problems are often the first sign of more serious health conditions. We know that our bodies shut down digestion as part of its stress response. This is so that it can divert the energy needed to digest food to more immediate safety concerns. Noticing things like heartburn, cramping, diarrhea, or constipation can be clues that our bodies are under stress. So it's important to intentionally check in on this.

- *Beyond my body's processing of food, am I also giving my body opportunities to move throughout the day?*

For some people, this includes a structured exercise schedule. For others, just allowing for short walks between clients might be important.

The last biological area I check in on is general physical health.

- *Do I have any chronic or acute health conditions that I need to tend to?*
- *Am I engaged in regular preventive medical appointments? Even something as simple as getting my teeth cleaned twice a year at the dentist counts here.*
- *Am I taking any prescribed medication as directed?*

Psychological

- *How is my mental health?*
- *Am I feeling any symptoms of depression, or anxiety, which are the two conditions I have been diagnosed with?*

For students and clients, any mental health diagnoses need to be addressed. I encourage students to take a self-administered depression or anxiety questionnaire, like the PHQ-9 or the GAD-7, to self-assess every few months. These are two standardized measures commonly given during medical appointments, and people can track their scores to monitor their symptoms.

Also, for any students or counselors who are in recovery, it is important to assess how their program of recovery is going.

- *How stable is my sobriety?*
- *Am I attending regular self-help groups or otherwise attending to my recovery needs?*
- *Beyond any diagnosed mental health conditions, how I am handling stress in general? All counseling jobs are stressful. Do I have the energy and ability to address the daily stresses that are occurring? Or am I getting overwhelmed regularly?*

We know that when stress goes up, executive brain functioning goes down. For people who work in stressful jobs, we must intentionally refuel our executive tanks.

Many counselors have found it helpful to seek their own therapy, and it is something I strongly encourage.

Social

- *How are the relationships in my life?*
- *Do I have consistent sources of social support?*
- *Am I able to attend to all my social roles—as daughter, sister, wife, friend, etc.?*
- *Are my relationships balanced, so that I am both giving and receiving support?*

Some people have deeper social needs than others, and it's important to pay attention to each of our own unique needs here. For some people, an active and varied social life brings joy and connection; for others, having a small circle of deep connections is better. Understanding one's extroversion and introversion needs here is critical.

- *And again, are my relationships balanced, allowing me to both give and receive support? Counselors are, by profession, focused on helping others. We have a tendency to do this in our personal lives, too, being the source of support for others and not allowing others to be sources of support to us.*

Spiritual

- *Here, I am assessing for a sense of meaning and purpose in life.*
- *Do I feel connected to something bigger than myself?*
- *Do I feel my life has meaning?*
- *Do I feel connected to a higher purpose?*
- *Am I engaged in activities that strengthen these?*
- *For people with an ascribed religious practice: Am I feeling fulfilled in this area?*

I call this bio-psycho-social-spiritual scan my *self-care dashboard*. Breaking the concept of self-care into these four core areas helps me see where I am doing well, and where I need to bring more focus.

I also ascribe to the progress-not-perfection principle when it comes to self-care. No one has a perfect self-care regimen. We all always have areas we could improve upon. And I am by no means superior to anyone else who struggles with self-care. Once, I let myself get run down pretty bad. I had been experiencing digestive issues for several months, but I didn't listen to my body and pushed forward. I ended up in the hospital and needed an emergency gall-bladder removal surgery. My call for students and counselors to focus regularly on this is also a reminder for me to do so as well.

Wounded 15

Miami

Just after my two-month mark of sobriety, I had a business trip to Miami. I typically had to travel for work several times a year, presenting at conferences or attending trainings. After what had happened the summer before in Atlanta at the AA World Convention, I was extremely anxious about this trip. In the past, whenever I travelled alone, I always used. It was a perfect setup. No one would ever know. I had done it many times before.

The previous two months had been hard. Anyone in early recovery will tell you that just getting through the normal tasks of a day without using requires an enormous amount of psychological and emotional energy.

The day after my last use, I contacted a local treatment center that I'd never had any contacts with through my job. I went in for an assessment. Once again, they didn't know what to do with me. I was someone who was drinking two to three drinks a few days a week—on the surface, hardly something that would get recommended for treatment. I asked them to enroll me in an intensive outpatient group. This level of care involved 12 hours of treatment per week, usually four three-hour groups a week, led by an addiction counselor. I chose one that met in the evenings, so I didn't have to take time away from my job.

As part of outpatient treatment, clients are often given assignments to do between sessions. This might include making a list of consequences, or completing worksheets on uncovering hidden irrational thoughts. The actual treatment work wasn't very helpful to me. I could do these things in my sleep. However, having a group of peers to talk to, to reflect on my progress with, was immensely helpful. I checked in faithfully each week, and talked openly and honestly. My counselor didn't really know how to connect with me. I clearly had years more training and knowledge about addiction and recovery treatment. But the process of humbling myself to the group—and putting forward my best, vulnerable effort—was working.

It was a very strange experience, going through treatment this time. The program I attended used a lot of the Hazelden Betty Ford treatment materials, including a lot of their educational videos. These videos included clips of interviews with experts from Hazelden. I would go to the large group room, sit in a semicircle with my fellow recovering peers, and watch a video about things like post-acute withdrawal syndrome, or setting boundaries in recovery. I would be following along, and suddenly, there was a counselor I used to work with talking about the neurobiology of addiction. The next week, I watched an interview with a unit supervisor I worked closely with. It was surreal to sit in a room with other patients watching videos of my coworkers—some of whom I had worked quite closely—deliver psychoeducation on addiction topics.

The Miami trip occurred about eight weeks into this treatment. I acquired special permission to miss two days of treatment. I flew out on a Wednesday afternoon. The cravings started as I walked past the airport bar. They filtered up through my consciousness and began to form ludicrous thoughts. *What if*, I thought, *I checked into the hotel in Miami and scoped out a local pharmacy. I could buy a package of Benadryl and use Friday night after the conference.* To cover my tracks, I thought I'd even find a local AA meeting to attend first and make sure I told my sponsor and Sarah I was going. It was a fleeting thought, but as the plane curved southward toward Miami, soon my mind could not think of anything else. I found myself visualizing, over and over, walking to a local pharmacy, entering the store, and finding the allergy medication aisle.

I could see my hand reaching out, picking up a box, then checking out at the register. I could see myself walking back to the hotel, entering my room, and getting each pill out of the blister pack. I imagined swallowing the pills and collapsing into the hotel bed to wait for oblivion.

By the time the plane landed, the craving had taken over. I was committed to this relapse. I'd have to wait a day to set everything in motion (I did have a conference to attend, after all), but I would do it. Once I arrived at the hotel, I did an online search for local pharmacies. There was a CVS a few blocks away.

I located an AA meeting that met on Friday night to use as cover. I prepared my cover story, complete with fake details and asides. And then the funniest thing happened. I called the following afternoon to check in with Sarah, to see how she was and to set my alibi in motion. Turns out she was at the tire store. My car had been needing new tires, and she had taken the day off to get them put on early, as a surprise. As we talked, a jolt suddenly flashed through my body. I was yanked out of my craving. When I was on the phone with her, I very clearly saw what I was about to do. Here was this woman, giving her afternoon and showing me love by getting my car new tires, and I was about to repay her by relapsing. I couldn't possibly do that to her. I didn't care about what a relapse would do to me, but I couldn't hurt her like that. When I got off the phone, I called my sponsor and confessed my plan.

The rest of the day was a blur. Instead of using that night, I ended up at an AA meeting on Miami Beach. It was a small group, only five people or so, who all knew each other well. They welcomed me. I opened up and confessed what I had planned to do, what I no longer wanted to do. I asked for help. The group had a tradition of going out to dinner after the meeting and invited me to join them. I did, and I had a lovely dinner, but I was still wary about returning to the hotel room. I didn't trust myself.

The second I stepped through the door, I called my sister. I told her what my original plan was, and she stayed on the phone with me, chatting with me about mundane things until I fell asleep.

The next morning, I woke up amazed. Yesterday, I had easily been 80 percent of the way to using. In the past, once I had the initial thought, it was a done deal. A thought would occur, and I *always* ended up acting on it. Even if the initial thought was only 5 percent of the way to using, I would always lose. Sometimes it took few minutes, sometimes a few hours, but the craving always won. For decades, it had been the only reality I knew. But this time, I hadn't used. I'd stopped myself by talking and asking for help. I could not believe I could come that close to using, and then change my course. For the first time in 30 years, I was able to do something different. I had been successful at beating a craving. I hugged myself as I continued to wake up, congratulating myself on this major victory.

This event was a major milestone in my recovery. From that day on, I knew that I had the power to beat a craving. My psychiatrist laughed with glee and clapped her hands when I told her the story during my next appointment. "Love," she said, "that's what stopped you."

Healing 26

Surfing

Now that I'm in stable recovery, my days mostly flow fairly easily. But there are days when I get overwhelmed. I am able to lead a very busy life, and I have influence in so many ways. This brings tremendous power and privilege, which I try to open up and pass on to others. But it also means my days tend to be packed. I've come to find that in recovery, I tend to exist in one of two states: either I'm on top of the surfboard riding the wave of life, or I'm getting sucked down under its undertow.

In 12-step recovery, there is a concept called living on life's terms. We work in recovery to move through life in such a way that we are going with the flow of what our lives are bringing to us. This involves acceptance of whatever is unfolding, and responding in a way that is appropriate and responsible. When I am able to do this, it feels like a surfer feels when they catch a wave. This analogy works for me for a number of reasons.

First, consider the surfboard. Surfers will tell you it's important to take care of your board. Storing it properly, keeping it out of sun and heat, repairing small dings before they get too big, rinsing with water after use, and keeping it properly waxed can extend the life of the board. Similarly, people need to engage in self-care to keep themselves in top shape. You can't surf a wave without a board, and you can't live life on life's terms if you're not taking care of yourself. When I'm surfing in life, I'm doing all the things I need to do to take care of myself.

Remain present. One thing that will knock surfers off a good ride is if they become too caught up in their thoughts. A good ride involves clearing the mind of all chatter, and focusing only on the wave you're on. At the same time, surfers can't be overly focused on any part of what they're doing. When you start thinking about whether your knees are bent enough or how you're holding your arms, you lose your connection to the wave. A presence is required, but not an over-analyzing. Similarly in life, we need to be attuned to what is happening around us in the present moment. When I'm surfing in life, I am able to focus on whatever is right in front of me. I don't go through the day replaying earlier events or worrying about the future. When I'm really surfing, I feel at one with the world. I feel utterly connected to my surroundings. I can feel the energy of life pulsing within and all around me.

Use proper paddling technique, and keep a trim board. Your body needs to be on the board in the correct position to create the correct angle of the board in the water. If the angle is too low, the nose of the surfboard will go under the water, impeding your forward progress. Similarly, if the angle is too high, you will waste energy in your arm strokes and not move forward. Keeping the nose a few degrees above horizontal maximizes the energy transmission from your arms to the water. Similarly, I have to engage in life in a way that maintains good "surfing posture." If I'm trying to do too much or with too little help, it's like trying to paddle with the board angle too high; I'm expending all this effort, but I'm not making efficient progress on anything. I have to take on the right levels of the right kinds of commitments to keep my board angle correct.

Your head is your steering wheel. Surfing guides will tell you the proper sequence for turning a surfboard is first turning your head and looking at where you want to go, and then letting that action propagate down your body, finishing with your feet. Most people think that the action initiates with the feet, but it all starts with visual intention. When I'm surfing in life, I'm mindful and intentional, instead of getting pulled in all directions.

When I can do all these things—take care of my board, remain present, use proper paddling technique, and turn my course appropriately—I enter the *flow state*. This psychological state was first described by Mihály Csíkszentmihályi in his study of artists who he found could enter a state of oneness with their painting. It's been studied in many high-performing areas including music, sports, and gaming. And it's been heavily studied in occupational psychology. People who have been able to achieve the flow state feel they are performing optimally.

So, when I'm in a flow state, life is great. I'm engaged, active, and responsive. But things can knock me off my board. Putting too much on my plate, an unexpected life event, getting sick, things like this can rip me out of the flow state in a heartbeat. And then I can feel myself falling off my surfboard, the power of the wave sucking me under the board. I experience the turbulence of the water, and feel the sting of the salt. I metaphorically flounder, wildly flailing my arms and legs while trying to reach equilibrium again. It is a very distressing experience.

When I sense this has happened, I do what I must do to get my head above water again. And I've learned that the only way to get back to flow is to focus on those fundamentals. I get my surfboard back in shape with a period of self-care. I work through whatever emotions and reactions are keeping me in my head and preventing me from experiencing the present. I reenter my schedules and routines and adjust what needs to be adjusted, shifting priorities and matching my output with my often reduced abilities. I detach from the directions others are demanding, and put my intention into what I need to do next. I can never get back into flow by wishing for it to happen, or trying to will it back into existence. But when I let go of trying to make it happen and focus on those fundamentals, it reemerges all on its own.

Above all else, I must accept there will always be waves. It is impossible to live a life with no waves. Life *is* waves. The only choice we have is to learn how to surf them, or be continually pulled under by them. Some days the waves are bigger than others, but we can only ride the wave that we are given. At the same time, we have some choice about which waves we choose to ride. We don't have to ride every wave. And other people may try to get us to hop onto their wave, but we must maintain focus on our waves. I now use the surfing analogy frequently in the counseling and teaching that I do. Having this visual seems to help people understand the concepts.

Finally, I've learned that the only way to learn how to surf is to get out there on a board. People who are good at surfing have spent hundreds to thousands of hours paddling out, catching waves, falling, recovering, and paddling back out. There is no substitute for learning how to live life, other than to live it. Falling off the board is part of learning how to surf. It teaches us how to handle the next wave. And all surfers will occasionally fall off their board. Nobody surfs every wave perfectly. The whole purpose of counseling is to help people chose the right waves for them, and to teach them proper technique. And I feel a special kind of vicarious joy when other people get into their own flow state.

Healing 27

The Year of the Promises

All 12-step recovery meetings include a set of readings to begin or end each meeting. They serve as an introduction to the newcomer and a reminder to everyone of the focus of the meeting. Brief passages of the *Big Book*, or whatever basic text the fellowship uses, describe the program and who it is for. Usually the 12 Steps are read. Sometimes the 12 Traditions are read. And many groups read something called the Promises.

The Promises are a group of 12 statements that the founders of AA believed would come true for an individual who works the 12 steps. In the *Big Book*, they are specifically placed after the instructions for step nine, which is where the individual goes and makes amends wherever possible to any people they have hurt in the course of their life.

The reason the Promises are often read at meetings is to provide hope and optimism to people who are just getting sober; this is usually a time of great distress, discomfort, and shame. I remember sitting in meetings for years listening to them being read, and hearing people in recovery attesting to their truth. Personally, I looked at the list with more than a healthy dose of skepticism. Knowing what I knew about myself and thinking about everything I had experienced in my life, I felt there was little chance that they would ever come true for me. But year after year, I listened to people speak about how they had come true for them, so somewhere inside me was the tiniest sliver of hope that one day, maybe, I would experience them, too.

For the first three years of my sobriety, I mainly attended two 12-step groups, neither of which read the Promises as a regular part of their meeting regimen. As a result, they faded from my memory, and I gave them little thought. I worked the program of recovery as directed. My day-to-day experience of recovery was one of slow but steady growth.

And then winter one day about 3.5 years in, I was sitting at my desk at work. As I was switching tasks, I glanced up and looked out at the snow outside my office window. I suddenly became aware that my mood was good, pretty happy even. I became aware that life wasn't taking all this effort like it used to. I felt light, and contented. As my awareness focused, I understood that my depression had totally lifted. And then I suddenly remembered the Promises. I quickly pulled them up in a web browser and read them one by one. I sat there with my jaw open. Over the past year, each one had come true.

Here they are, along with how I saw them in my life.

We Are Going to Know a New Freedom and a New Happiness

I did feel free indeed. There was a sense of play to my life that had never been there before. I felt free to move about and experience life as it presented itself, with a belief that I was capable of dealing with whatever it brought. For the first time ever, I *liked* my life. For decades, my daily experience had been to move between a set of tasks, each designed to prove to the people around me that I was good enough. Everything I did in my work, everything I did in my relationships, was to serve this larger purpose: *please like me, and tell me that I'm okay*. But I no longer structured my days this way. Life was not a series of events where I desperately wanted other people to like and accept me. Life was now fun. It was interesting, a series of adventures to enjoy.

We Will Not Regret the Past Nor Wish to Shut the Door on It

I could see how every second of my life had contributed to where I was now, at this moment. Nothing—no experience, no relationship, nothing in my life—had been wasted. All the hardships, all the failures, all of it was necessary to produce who I was now. And I no longer felt the need to hide all the things I had been through from other people. Before, I'd kept my past struggles hidden, only sharing the parts of my life where I had been successful and mentally well (and let me tell you, there was a lot of smoke and mirrors involved here). Now, I no longer felt shame in what I had been through. In fact, I *wanted* to share it with other people. And I remained acutely aware of what the hardships had taught me. I didn't wish to experience life as a new path, distancing myself from what I had been through and leaving it behind. Instead, every day, my life was informed by *all* I had been through. I had developed a gratitude and appreciation for my past.

We Will Comprehend the Word *Serenity*, and We Will Know Peace

I did indeed have this Zen feeling about me. I had developed a trust that the universe would take care of me. I did not need to worry or fret about anything. Whatever I needed would appear, and I was capable of being okay if it didn't appear. I knew that there would be future hardships, but they would only present themselves when I was ready, and the resources I needed to overcome them would also appear.

No Matter How Far Down the Scale We Have Gone, We Will See How Our Experience Can Benefit Others

This one held particular meaning for me as a person in recovery from an eating disorder. I really don't know what "scale" the alcoholics were referring to, but every time I read this, I could only think about my weight. And it was true that no matter what number appeared on my bathroom scale, I knew that I had the capacity to help others through what I had learned.

That Feeling of Uselessness and Self-Pity Will Disappear

Just a few months prior, I had been up for a promotion to associate professor. This involved putting together an extensive portfolio of all I had done in my career, documenting all the contributions I had made to the school that warranted recognition with a promotion. I put it together, but very anxiously. I genuinely felt like I didn't deserve the promotion. I couldn't see how much I had contributed. If someone had asked me, I would have shrugged and said I was probably below average as a professor. This was never reflected by my colleagues; they all said I was a shoo-in. But now . . . now I felt very useful. I saw my worth. I could recognize that I was a good teacher, and a good counselor. I had unique talents. I also saw my worth as a friend, and as a wife. And I didn't need others to tell me all this; I knew it deeply on my own.

We Will Lose Interest in Selfish Things and Gain Interest in Our Fellow

My old way of operating was pretty much to look out for *numero uno*. I was only interested in what I could get out of a situation. Everything I did for others was always done with a what's-in-it-for-me attitude. If I couldn't benefit in some way, I would look to reduce my effort or commitment. Looking back, I realize this is because I only had enough energy to barely get my needs met. But now I was regularly prioritizing the needs of others. I would go the extra mile for the student or do the something extra special for my wife. I would raise my hand to show interest in being a sponsor at meetings and truly mean it. I genuinely wanted to make other people's lives better.

Self-Seeking Will Slip Away

I had to admit, this is the one promise that I'm still working on. I still do make choices that seek to highlight me over others. I'll still fish for compliments from students, coworkers, and clients. It's gotten a lot better, to be sure, but I am still selfish in this and other ways.

Our Whole Attitude and Outlook Upon Life Will Change

My expectations of life had always been pretty bleak. Really, I just hoped that I would not suffer too much. I used to wake up each day with a feeling of dread, thinking, *What's the bare minimum I need to do to get through the day?* I really never thought that life could be fun. But it was. Now I wake up each morning rested, excited about the day's possibilities. I looked forward to seeing people and doing things.

Fear of People and of Economic Insecurity Will Leave Us

Of all the promises, this is the one I was positive would never come true for me. I didn't even try to have hope. And yet, as I read it that day, I could see that it had.

I used to experience everyone from a place of fear. Fear of what they were thinking of me. Fear of disappointing them. Fear of rejection from them. I crafted all my interactions with people to minimize any experience of this. I said as little as possible, and I asked little of others. This pretty deep fear had been cemented during middle school when I experienced my social trauma.

But I could see I no longer had any of these fears. Now, I was genuinely interested in people. I wanted to learn what they were thinking and how they were experiencing different things. I was fascinated and drawn to people. My fear had been replaced with curiosity.

I had also spent my entire life feeling insecure financially. I was always worried that I would never have enough money. I had spent years as a poor graduate student while other people were building up their 401Ks. I never had enough money to pay all my bills. I always had to choose substandard housing, because that's all I could afford. The possibility of becoming a homeowner was completely foreign to me. I was reckless in my spending when I was active in my addiction. I entered sobriety with $20,000 in credit card debt and $100,000 in student loans. I never put money in savings. But now, I was starting to get a handle on things. I had consolidated my credit card debt, and was about 18 months from paying it off. I hadn't accumulated any new debt for years. I was enrolled in a public service loan forgiveness program that I would meet requirements for in a couple of years. At the end of each month, I actually had a little money left over. But more than that, I had developed a deep internal belief that I didn't need to worry about money anymore. I had the means and the ability to hustle if I needed to.

We Will Intuitively Know How to Handle Situations Which Used to Baffle Us

I used to move through life so tentative and unsure. I questioned most everything I did. I never felt like I knew what to do. And no matter what I did, I constantly questioned it afterward. *Was it right? Was it okay? I probably should have done that differently.* But now, I was routinely walking into challenging situations, and a solution would bubble up into my consciousness. I could weigh different options and confidently walk through problems with responses that maximized benefits for those involved. I collaborated with people to get different viewpoints; I compromised when necessary. I regularly doubled back and checked how the solution was working for everyone, making adjustments as needed.

We Will Suddenly Realize That Our Higher Power Is Doing for Us What We Could Not Do for Ourselves

Even now when I read this, this promise doesn't quite resonate for me. I don't view my Higher Power as a "something" that does "anything." But I can recognize that I feel connected to people around me, and when I make myself vulnerable and ask for help, it is usually there. I know there is truly little I can do all on my own.

That day, I sat back after reading the last promise on the computer screen, amazed. These statements, which I had been reading for 15 years—always hopeful but in reality doubtful—had happened. Since then, I've come to understand that we don't reach a point in our lives where the promises "turn on," allowing us to live the rest of our lives under their glow. With the ups and downs of life, we slide back and forth along the continuum of promises, feeling them more some days than others. And I don't think we get them because we aim for them. We can't make a goal to lower our feelings of uselessness or increase our interest in others. Instead, they appear as a natural byproduct of healing. By jumping in and doing the deep work, when we come back to the surface, they are there for us.

I've also found that the Promises aren't limited to recovery from addiction. I've seen them come true for my non-addicted clients whose issues ranged from abuse to overcoming an anxiety disorder. One client I worked with was diagnosed with PTSD after leaving an abusive marriage. For 18 months, we met, and she worked to overcome the effects of her trauma. Slowly but surely, she began to experience success. I saw her return to life. One day, toward the end of our work, I brought in the Promises and had her read them and reflect on them. I didn't tell her at first where they came from. She read them slowly, tentatively at first, and then with more confidence as she identified with each statement. I saw a smile appear at the corners of her mouth as she recognized her new self on the page. When she was done reading, she looked up at me, incredulous.

"How did this happen?" she asked.

"I can't tell you for certain," I said. "I just know this is what happens to people when they truly heal."

Wounded 16

The Next Layer

Although I've come a long way, I'm still a work in progress. Peggy taught me early on that healing is less like a walking a linear path and more like peeling layers, like of an onion. You can only deal with the layer that has presented itself. And we can trust ourselves that whatever layer emerges is the one we are ready to work on. In addition, that layer can patiently wait. We get to choose when to work on a layer. It will continue to present itself in different ways in our lives until we are ready. And once we've worked through that layer, the next one that is ready will emerge. We can trust this process.

Over the past two decades, I have trusted. I've overcome my codependency, my shame disorder, my eating disorder, and my substance use disorder, but I still struggle with a number of issues. My current layer has to do with feeling comfortable in my body.

I've never been a physically demonstrative person. No one in my family was. I don't remember cuddles as a child or hugs when I was struggling. The only time my mother would touch me was when she was playfully making a point. She would reach out to give a rough pat on my arm; I flinched every time.

So for me, 12-step recovery meetings posed a danger. People in NA famously say, "Hugs, not drugs." A hug is the common greeting and goodbye at every meeting. And not just one or two hugs. I'd have to hug everyone in the meeting, usually 10 to 20 people. I've worked a lot on being comfortable with hugs, but it still feels unnatural to me.

My wife loves having her back scratched. She freely asks for this all the time. I love it too, especially before I go to sleep, but I have a difficult time asking her to do this. Instead, I keep a long, wooden back scratcher by my bed for nightly use, because I find it too difficult to ask for a back scratch. Allowing someone, even my wife, to touch my body feels uncomfortable.

The first year my wife and I were dating, she gave me a Groupon for a massage for my birthday. It was a loving gesture. I have always been curious about getting a massage, but have never been able to get one. They are frequently recommended to all mental health professionals, as we often let in the negative energy of our clients into our bodies, and massages help channel this energy out. But the thought of some stranger touching my body does not in any way sound relaxing to me. So I wish I could be a person who enjoys a message, but I've got a way to go. I keep the Groupon on the fridge to remind myself of this goal. It's been nine years. Maybe one day I will be able to get one.

I suspect that over the next decade, the next phase of my healing will involve a great deal of body work around physical intimacy. I've slowly noticed myself warming to the idea. I know I don't have to force it to happen, and I certainly don't have to shame myself for not being ready. So I remain open, waiting for my body to signal it's time to do the work.

My experiences with healing have given me reverence for my clients' timelines for healing. I understand that their healing also happens in layers, and that we can respect and honor any non-readiness to do the work. The students I teach often feel the need to force recovery or healing onto their clients according to their own timelines. This wish comes from a place of care and concern, but it is misdirected energy. When we fail to honor our clients' resistance, we are not really helping them, but rather mapping our will onto them. Healing can't occur under those conditions.

Our real jobs are to see, accept, and join. And trust the process.

Healing 28

The Hero's Journey

In 1949, a literature professor named Joseph Campbell published a famous book called *The Hero with a Thousand Faces*. His specialty was comparative mythology and comparative religion, in that he looked for commonalities in the myths and religious stories from cultures all over the world and through all of time. He found and presented evidence for what he called a monomyth, or universal myth, and named it "The Hero's Journey." He outlines dozens of examples of this myth, from Greek mythology to Christian, Hindu, and Buddhist religions, to Aztec and Inuit stories. Since then, writers have found evidence of the Hero's Journey myth in much of modern literature and cinema, most notably the film *Star Wars*.

Campbell describes common elements of the hero's journey in an elaborate 17 stages. The story always starts out with a person, usually a man, whom we meet in his everyday life. This man experiences some kind of "call to adventure," whereby he is asked to leave the world of the known to venture into the world of the supernatural or unknown. Often he resists this call and is aided in engaging by some deity or spirit. Once he accepts the call, he enters an unknown world and has to confront a number of tests or challenges. He experiences doubt and fear, and must overcome these as well. Setbacks abound, requiring faith and endurance on the part of the hero, and he is usually given help by some kind of spiritual guide. He often must give up some part of himself to achieve victory. Ultimately, he succeeds and is given access to a powerful truth or object. He steps beyond his individual self and is given the power to see beyond life and death. He somehow confronts the universal fear of death, often represented by a male deity, and is freed from its grips. He is tempted to wallow forever in this bliss, and must make a choice to return to the world of the living. The return trip is also riddled with obstacles and challenges. Ultimately, the hero returns to the known world, bringing his treasured knowledge or item to share with his community.

Campbell argues that the monomyth exists to explain the universal human experience of living. We are born, then must separate and individuate from our caregivers and progress through the challenges of life, ascending from the individual ego to a spiritual plane. The monomyth serves to communicate this universal journey to children to prepare them for their lives. In a way, it serves as a primitive psychology.

In his book, Campbell makes many connections to Jungian psychology, which was the prominent psychological theory at the time. Jung argued that archetypes exist in our psyches—drawn from our collective unconscious—that manifest in art and literature. These include the archetypes of creator, ruler, hero, everyman, jester, and sage. So both Campbell and Jung argue that there is some imprint upon the human mind to impose these archetypes on the world as a means of understanding it. In short, we seemed to be wired to organize our experiences in life this way.

Campbell's argument of the monomyth is not without critics. But I often find myself thinking about the Hero's Journey when I'm working with clients. In many ways, I can see the process and experience of therapy itself is its own hero's journey. Clients encounter some event or experience in their lives that cause distress. As a result, they are called to enter the supernatural space of therapy. There, they are guided by the knowing therapist through a number of challenges, most notably confronting their own fears and setbacks. Ideally, they overcome the challenges and reach a place of self-knowledge and peace.

The therapist then returns the client to their world with this newfound knowledge to engage differently with people in their lives. I try to be mindful that each client is on their own hero's journey and respect the various stages the journey requires.

I especially see the hero's journey motif in the recovery process for individuals with substance use disorders. Here, the metaphorical demons addicts face must be conquered for true and lasting recovery. People in recovery are transformed by the journey from resentful, fearful, destructive beings to accepting, serene, connected individuals who go on to share their newfound existence with others.

My own recovery definitely follows the motif. I spent 11 years refusing the call to adventure, but once I did, I entered a space that definitely felt supernatural. I was immersed in this space for about three years, and I had to fight and overcome all my blocks to living. I was aided by the guidance of others and transcended my physical existence to understand some universal truths. My most notable demons were shame and fear. I was given the gifts of self-acceptance and connection. Over time, these transformed me, and I began to see the world through a different lens. Now that I have returned to life, I venture to share what I've learned with others.

I must say, it is a very surreal thing to know that I have become a guide for others, but I think that's the ultimate end of the hero's journey.

Wounded 17

The Dad Chapter

When authors take on a big project like a book, the first draft is never the one that gets published. Writers often spend months, even years, structuring, writing, and revising. This manuscript accordingly went through several drafts. I collected chapter ideas here and there in a list for about six months in my phone, and then spent 18 months typing out the first draft whenever I could find a few hours at a time. It produced a manuscript that was about 70 percent of the way the book you are reading now is. A solid first effort.

At this point, it was very important to me to get my family members' feedback on what I had written, as revealing my story meant revealing some of theirs. I wanted them to be okay with that, and to talk to me if they weren't, so we could decide what to do. I had been talking throughout my writing to my two sisters, mother, and father in a general way about what I was writing, but finally it was time for them to see my words.

I chose to get my two sisters' feedback first. I was closest to them, and they had experienced much of the same childhood as I had. But I'd hidden most of my addicted adult life from them. This book would be revealing a lot more than they had ever known about me. I knew some things were going to be hard for them to read; I had never talked about my suicide attempt or most of the things I had done in my addiction. I tried to prepare them the best I could. I let them know that I was prepared for any reaction, and was willing to talk about any aspect of the book they wanted to. If they wanted more information on something that happened to me, I was game to tell them. If they wanted to counter some memory of mine, I wanted to hear it. If they wanted to process their experiences of my addiction, I was open. But I'll admit my heart quickened and my breath went shallow when I hit the send button on that email. I. was. nervous. Besides my wife, I hadn't let anyone who wasn't a member of AA or NA see the deepest inner guts of my life. I didn't know how they were going to respond. I wasn't sure if they were going to be angry, or shocked, or sad, or shaming, about what I had written. I had flashes of all possible reactions running through my head.

It turns out they both had the same reaction, and I was completely caught off guard by it. They both shared surprise and shock at something I *hadn't* written about. "Why was our dad hardly anywhere in the book?" they asked. I thought I *had* written about him, but upon review, there wasn't really much about him. "You wrote a whole long chapter on mom," they said; they both thought it was completely unfair to write about mom like that and not about dad. They were actually quite angry about it. "He loomed so large in our lives," they said, "that it's wrong for you not to talk about that."

I spent some time reflecting on this feedback. Most of this book was written from a powerful inner drive to tell my story of addiction and share what I'd learned in working with others. Many of the chapters just poured out of me from some deep inner well; sometimes I couldn't type fast enough to capture what was bubbling up. It was a process that was driven by something deep inside me. And I just trusted the process and wrote what was surfacing. The mom chapter was produced in this way. I would awake in the morning and discover my mind had been writing sentences and paragraphs in the space between asleep and awake. Most of the first draft was written this way. And dad had just not been a part of this process.

But they were right. Dad had loomed very large in our childhoods. But mostly by his absence.

Until last spring. On one March morning, I was about to go into a session with a client when my sister called. She left an urgent message that I needed to call her immediately. Two scenarios flashed in my mind: something had happened to her or our sister, or our father was dead. She was tearful as she described that dad had been found deceased on the kitchen floor of his North Carolina home that morning. He died of an apparent diabetic coma caused by excessive drinking. I was not surprised. I had been expecting this for some time.

I spent the next 10 days in North Carolina, helping to handle his arrangements with my sisters. It was a travel back in time for me, as I had not spent much time in his world in the past 2.5 decades. We talked about once a month, usually brief conversations highlighting things we had been working on, places we had traveled, or fun stories about people around us. But nothing too deep. Certainly nothing I discussed with those close to me. Being immersed back in his world so intensely for his funeral was jarring. But it's hard to understand what it was like without knowing more about his life.

As I moved through those 10 days in North Carolina, I understood why I hadn't written much about dad. It hadn't been time yet. But now it was. So much was surfacing for me, bubbling up the same way the rest of this book had, and becoming connected to what I had written about.

My dad was born in his childhood home toward the end of World War II, the second son of a shrimper and housewife on the coast of North Carolina. He spent his childhood working on my grandfather's shrimp boat, cementing a love of the sea that had endured in our family for generations (this continues in me today). He described a tightly restricted childhood with little freedom. He was not allowed to go anywhere but home and school, and he was not allowed to date. His escapes were sports and academics, so he joined as many teams as possible. He received a scholarship to attend college at the University of North Carolina in Chapel Hill, located a world away from his rural fishing village.

The freedom my father said he experienced once he went to college was overwhelming, and with no external restraints, he let loose in a big way. It was here that he began pursuing a life of pleasure. This led to him losing his scholarship, but his childhood work ethic allowed him to support himself in other ways. His sophomore year, he met my mother; they married, and she also worked to support him. He went on to law school and soon graduated and passed the bar. They returned home to a nearby county, and he began his legal career, first as a county prosecutor, before moving into his own law practice as a defense attorney. I and my two sisters were born, and he slowly gained reputation, influence, and wealth. When I was in middle school, he was elected to the North Carolina Senate and served two terms. In our small pond, he was a pretty big fish. From the outside, it seemed like the life of a successful and happy person.

But underneath the façade of a well-functioning family, a world of turmoil was churning. In my adulthood, a slow trickle of stories allowed me to piece together what I think was happening under the surface. Here is my best guess.

The unrestricted freedom my father tasted in his first two years of college was seducing. He spent a lot of time partying and, I imagine, dating, two freedoms he didn't want to give up when he married my mom. When they married, apparently he asked her for an open marriage, which she staunchly rejected. My dad didn't like this response, so he just decided to continue his pursuit of pleasure in secret.

My parents were married 32 years. When they separated in my early 20s, my dad's secret romantic life surfaced. He'd had many, many affairs. He disguised many of his trysts as hunting trips, some of which were legit, many of which were simply cover. His final affair was with a woman he met during his Senate service, whom he carried on with during the six months per year he lived in the state capitol. All my sisters and I knew during our childhood was that he was gone about as much as he was home.

And I think we had all unconsciously internalized his absence as some failing on our part. When I think back on my relationship with my dad during my childhood, all I remember is a deep, intense yearning that he would be with us. And I think this drove me to succeed, in an attempt to get a sliver of his attention and praise. I'm sure my sisters did this as well in their own ways.

But it also seemed my dad had only attention for one of us at a time, and this produced a competition between us. It was like Dad only had one beam to his spotlight, and when that spotlight was focused on you, you felt like the most special thing in the world. But just outside the spotlight, in the shadows, were my sisters who were trying to get the spotlight focused on them. It was always clear to us who was his favorite at any given time, and it was our job to shove that person out of the way and take over the spotlight. This rivalry colored our childhood and adolescent relationships.

Another reason none of us felt we were good enough for Dad is because we all had the unfortunate gall to be girls. It was very apparent that Dad had really wanted to have a boy, a son to father with lessons on hunting and gunsmithing and all the boy things. In retrospect, I suppose he was wanting to create a corrective experience from his restrictive boyhood, but alas, fate dealt him three girls. His response was to do all the boy stuff with us anyway. So we were raised knowing how to shoot a gun, ride four-wheelers, throw axes, and shake hands. These lessons were absorbed to varying degrees among us. But as we matured into adolescence, my older sister and I shifted into more girly interests. My younger sister, however, absorbed it all and formed a deeper connection and yearning for him.

We were also raised with very loose rules around relationships. My mother had set a rule that if anyone we were dating showed up on a motorcycle or in a van, we were not allowed to go, but my father was always more open to letting us have wild teenage experiences. Because he was a state senator, we were given a layer of legal privilege, so speeding or minor legal infractions were never a worry for us.

When I was a 15-year-old sophomore in high school, I started dating a senior. My parents planned a fabulous RV vacation that summer to Washington, DC, to celebrate July fourth on the Mall. We were allowed to bring someone; both my older sister and I brought our boyfriends. In DC, we stayed at a hotel. My dad paid for us to have our own suite. The hotel offered a free happy hour, and we were allowed to drink openly. I was floored that my father was facilitating a sexual relationship between us and our boyfriends, and letting us drink.

Dad himself spent most of the holiday drunk. I remember one raucous night when we went to a Greek restaurant. There were eight of us in the party. Dad sat at the head of the table. He picked up the menu upside down, and then moved it closer and further from his eyes, trying to read it, not knowing it wasn't right side up. Then the waiter came.

"Just bring one of everything on the menu," he slurred.

It was a bacchanalian feast, and most of us were along for the party. The whole weekend was conducted along these lines.

I was 20 years old when my parents split. I had been out of the house for about five years by then, having left to attend a residential science and math magnet school for my junior and senior years of high school, and then leaping directly to college from there. I was busy going through my own eating disorder and mental health challenges. When I found out my parents were splitting, honestly, my body experienced a deep wave of relief. *Finally, we can let go of the charade*, I thought. I somehow knew that we were not the shiny happy family that had always been portrayed outward. I didn't know the depths of our dysfunction, but on a subconscious level, I knew we were pretty messed up.

But my little sister had been more impacted. She had lived at home during the last few rocky years, including a failed attempt to leave when she was a junior in high school. Dad had been an absolute hero to her in childhood, and learning about his double life was devastating to her. We all tried to maintain contact with both him and Mom during and after the divorce process, to keep things fair. More and more of his doings were revealed. He decided to marry the last woman he was involved in an affair with, and she moved in with him on the farm.

I continued on with my life. I taught high school for a couple of years, and then my little sister and I decided to move to Chicago on a whim and start new lives. During our last weekend in North Carolina, we were out at a restaurant having dinner with Dad. He was particularly boisterous in describing some of the details of things he had done, including bragging that he had had "hundreds of affairs."

In an instant, my sister's desire to connect with him turned into bitter disappointment and disgust. She threw down her fork left the table. I found her in the parking lot. She said she was done with Dad. I didn't know what to do. I remember feeling a blank wave move through my body. I was frozen in my emotions. But I felt a loyalty to my sister, so I joined her in cutting off dad.

We packed up the moving truck the following day. We had been storing some things on the farm, so we had to go there to load up the truck. I remember the day was very hot, 98 degrees with 98 percent humidity. It was just the two of us, and we were exhausted at the end of packing. My sister wanted to return one of Dad's guns, and she left it on his kitchen table with a note saying, "I'm ashamed to have a father that is a liar, a cheater, and a thief. Goodbye." We got in the truck and drove away.

I maintained no contact with him for eight years, but I was always conflicted about it. As I began my journey of healing, it was inevitable that I was going to uncover my own dad issues in therapy. I did, and my therapist put them in the context of an addicted, dysfunctional family system. I began to see that my dad had actually lived a life of addictions. He didn't know it or have to face many consequences, because when one addiction would get out of hand, he would switch to another one. He cycled back and forth through various drinking, gambling, sex, spending, and work addictions year after year. He also exhibited some bipolar tendencies, sometimes going through depressed periods, and sometimes experiencing lavish and ludicrous times, like the trip to DC. I learned about codependent family systems, and how we had all participated and been affected.

As my understanding of my dad developed, I started talking to my therapist about reestablishing contact with him. But I needed to do it on my terms.

That spring, his 60th birthday was coming up. I decided to send a card with a brief note and an invitation to open up a line of written communication. He wrote back immediately. I could tell he was thrilled I had reached out. We exchanged letters for a year. Then I was ready for a phone call. We began talking once a month. Again, I could tell that this reestablished relationship meant a lot to him. I was living in Illinois with my partner and knew he wanted to visit. After six months of phone calls, I felt ready for this. I let him know that I was setting a boundary that I would not be around him if he were drinking, and that he had to agree to this if he was going to visit me. He did. We had a nice visit.

Getting to reestablish contact on my terms and having boundaries around my relationship with him, coupled with the deep work I was doing on codependency in therapy and Codependents Anonymous, provided the healing I needed. We settled into a new, adult relationship. We would visit in person every couple of years. Between these visits, we would have monthly phone calls, updating each other on our lives and celebrating or commiserating on the UNC Tarheels basketball team's performance. But I never felt very connected to him. I just didn't understand him.

However, Dad was not able to hold my boundary around not drinking around me. As he aged, he became a daily drinker, and I'm sure developed a severe alcohol use disorder. I maintained distance from this, both physically and psychologically. I realized it had become very severe the week he and the rest of my family came to participate in the family program at Caron, where I was receiving my own treatment for opioid use disorder.

He had driven up from North Carolina in a small RV he traveled in and planned to reside in it in the parking lot of the hotel the rest of my family was staying in. He drove it to the treatment center every day. At the end of one family therapy session, my sister told me she was with dad in the RV in the treatment center parking lot. He cracked a beer and started drinking in preparation for the drive to the hotel. My sister raised a concern, but he blew her off, feeling he was not doing anything wrong or unusual. When she told me about it, I passed on the information to my treatment team, who I believe had a conversation with him asking him not to drink on Caron property. I didn't hear anything else about it. But I knew what it meant when someone could not respect a boundary like that.

My dad divorced his second wife after about 15 years of marriage. He was getting much older now, in his 70s, and his health was declining. He had been dealing with diabetes since his 40s, and also had serious heart disease. This led to open heart surgery and a pacemaker.

My father was very shrewd. He made a calculated play for his third wife: he began dating a nurse who was 15 years younger than him. My sisters and I were sure this was his plan to avoid having to live in an old folks' home. With a younger nurse there to take care of him, he could live out his last few years in the comfort of his own home. Again, I couldn't understand this part of my dad. What kind of person would do something like this?

I do believe he came to love her, in the ways that he could. She became a traveling nurse, and they had grand adventures across the country. They bought a larger RV and would set up shop in Florida, or California, or another state for a few months at a time. My dad was an incredible people person. Wherever he went in his many travels, he could connect like nobody's business to locals. He thrilled in making these new connections and would often share stories about them in our calls.

There was just one problem. His new wife had a number of her own health problems. She had a history of her own substance use disorders, which were becoming more apparent to Dad over time.

A few months before they got married, he called me. In a serious tone, he described the extent of her use and asked for my professional opinion on what to do. I listened, and he shared he was concerned about whether or not he should marry her given her use. He had no insight into his own substance use disorder. I leaned on my professional training, with its ethical mandate not to treat family members, and recommended that she reach out to a local mental health professional who specializes in addiction and attend an assessment to determine what help she needed. I made the same recommendation for him. He was taken aback at this second recommendation, stating he did not have a problem like she had a problem. I could tell this was not the advice he was looking for.

He never spoke to me about her use again. They married that May. At the wedding, my dad made a point to gather my sisters and me for a private conversation in one corner of the reception. He shared with us that he had made her sign a prenup agreeing that each of their estates would go to their respective children. He wanted us to know that we were protected. He then asked flatly how long we should allow her to continue living in his house after he died before "we kicked her out so we could sell it."

My sisters and I flashed shock across our faces, stunned at such a cruel move on the day of his wedding. He actually thought this was going to please us, and he was going to bond with us over this. We quickly stated something along the lines of allowing her to live there as long as she wanted and ducked out of the conversation. We connected separately and shared our shock with one another. We'd done this a lot with dad over our lifetimes.

But it turns out the joke was on him. Two years later, she developed breast cancer and had to return to North Carolina for chemo and radiation. In the most ironic twist of his life, my father, who thought he had designed a foolproof plan to have someone take care of him, became the person who had to take care of her. My sisters and I discussed this irony openly. None of us ever talked to him about it.

As her health declined, both of them spiraled into very severe alcohol use disorders. He also had a standing prescription for OxyContin, which he took twice a day for some chronic pain issues. When he realized she was stealing it, he began to hide it around the farm in a locked box.

The May before he died, I visited him with Sarah. I noted a deep decline in his own physical health. He was now drinking every day, all day, and he was not taking care of his diabetes. My little sister had sent a very powerful letter to him a month before, sharing many of her memories of her life with him. They were not flattering. He wanted to talk to me about them, because this is not how he remembered his life with her at all.

Here was the heart-to-heart conversation I had been waiting all my life to have with him. He and I drove into town to run some errands and talked about everything. He shared extreme confusion over what my sister had reported; I confirmed many of the events as accurate. I shared some of my own as well—honestly, without blame or judgment. He urgently wanted me to understand his life, how he had been so restricted in his own childhood, and how this had led him to a life with no boundaries or restrictions. He never wanted his children to feel this way, so he never had many limits with us. I shared that I understood that.

I recounted an event one weekend when he had to take care of me and my sister on his own. He hooked up with a friend with a private plane, and they decided to engage in a weekend of debauchery during in Annapolis, Maryland during the Navy's fleet week. He took me and my sister along, and after we checked into the hotel room, gave us a bunch of cash and let us loose on the streets to find our dinner and have fun. I was 11. My sister was nine. I remember knowing this was more of an adult thing than I was ready for. My sister was terrified to be without the guidance of a parent. I just knew I needed to take care of her. The whole weekend went this way. We did our best, but the experience had a lasting impact on us.

I shared all of this with him. But he was incapable of taking this in. He was fixated on trying to get me to understand him.

As we concluded our errands and turned the car back toward the farm, I slowly accepted the fact that the heart-to-heart I had always wanted to have with him was not going to happen. He and I were never going to connect deeply. I felt sad, but okay. I knew I had some work to do to make peace with this fact, grieve it, and accept it, but I was capable of doing this on my own.

During this trip, his wife had an emergency. I found out later she was receiving medical treatment for her opioid use disorder with Suboxone replacement therapy. She was given control to self-administer her doses, but was taking them more frequently than prescribed. She experienced an overdose, and this was causing heart failure.

The night we arrived from the airport, I had to take her to the local ER for treatment. As her use was uncovered, Dad was given instructions to control the Suboxone dosing. I had another conversation with him encouraging both him and her to get a substance use disorder assessment and follow their recommendations. He shrugged off the suggestion. He acknowledged his severe use, but felt resigned to continuing his life as it was. On the last day of our trip, as we were pulling out of the driveway, I turned to my wife.

"I'm pretty sure I've just seen my dad alive for the last time," I said. She agreed this was probably the case.

I was right. He died the following March. I had already started my grief work after that trip, but his death, while not unexpected, was sudden. My sisters and I flew in from across the country and arrived at his home.

In the 1990s, my dad had purchased a 100-acre plot of farmland. In the proceeding years, he would sell off most of this land here and there to people who wanted to set up horse farms. This produced a patchwork of about nine mini horse farms and other properties. It had also created a small fiefdom that my father was king of. I could feel this fiefdom vibe every time I turned into the main driveway.

There was a tension to this fiefdom, however. My father, who had garnered great respect in his community, also engendered a lot of negative feelings. This worship-resentment tension was apparent everywhere. Over the course of a 45-year legal and political career that was combined with an uncanny ability to form relationships, my dad gained a lot of power and influence in the three counties he had lived in. He was connected to *everyone*. And he often used this power and influence to help out other people. But there was always a very clear, unspoken understanding that my father's generosity was always second to his self-interest. He was sharp and calculated in setting himself up for the best in any interaction. When you needed help, he was quick to offer it, but he would always attach some favor or cost you would owe him in return. In this way, the whole community that my dad had built was actually pretty sick, and I could feel these sick tentacles trying to wrap themselves around me with every conversation I had.

As people came to visit that week and attend the funeral, warm stories of my father's escapades were shared. All those who were along for the ride in my dad's pursuit of pleasure had a lot of good times. And a begrudging respect for the people game he played was also acknowledged multiple times, almost in an attempt to share their forgiveness for how my father had taken advantage of them. And, to be sure, Dad had never been subversive in his self-interest; he owned it. He almost seemed proud of it. Again, I could not understand this part of my father.

My sisters and I worked seamlessly in handling the funeral arrangements. Our talents and abilities complemented each other, and it turned out to be a week of deep bonding between us. One sister had experience handling estate issues after a sudden death; another had a financial background and knew most of the people in my dad's immediate orbit. I contributed by understanding and explaining the psychology of everything that was happening, soothing the uncertainties that arose. I also wrote and delivered the eulogy for his funeral. In it, I shared some of the shrewd life lessons he had taught me, such as teaching me how to drive, or how to examine any situation to determine what course of action to take. It was appropriately warm and modeled after my father's excellent storytelling.

I knew I was going to be the one who delivered the eulogy, because it just started to bubble up in me in the same way much of this book has. As the week we were there wore on, I'd be sitting on the couch or going for a walk, and a sentence would emerge in my head. I could feel the structure of a story form, and I started writing things down. Pretty soon, I had a 10-minute speech prepared. I proposed to everyone that I do the eulogy, and all agreed I was the best choice, especially given my comfort in public speaking. I shared the draft I had written with the family on the day before the funeral and incorporated their feedback. I kept in a line about him not winning any father of the year awards because this felt authentic, but I did not use the speech to settle any old scores. At this point, I had none.

But I will say that since the funeral, I've been surprised at how my relationship with him has continued to evolve. I had thought that his death meant where we were in our relationship was going to freeze. But the past year has actually brought about so many changes.

I returned to North Carolina with one sister a few months later to bury his cremated ashes in his chosen ancestral graveyard. Fitting for my dad, this was a cemetery that was only accessible by boat and required quite a bit of planning to pull off.

The week before I went, I suddenly remembered that my other sister had made a series of recordings of Dad about 15 years ago. She was the family's genealogist and did a bang-up professional job, including these recordings. I had never listened to them, but now I had a burning desire to. I emailed her, and she sent me about four hours of interviews with him, wherein he'd recounted his own life story along with many other family members. She also included two hours of interviews with his father, our grandfather. I downloaded them and listened to them as I commuted. As his voice came on, I felt a warmth rise in me. For all my father's faults, it was great to hear him talk and tell stories again.

As I listened to him sharing his life narrative from his viewpoint, I thought back to the way I had always conceptualized his life: as someone driven by the pursuit of pleasure and self-interest. But listening to his voice, I could now detect an undercurrent of something different, something sad. And then it came to me: my dad didn't pursue a life of pleasure; he was fleeing from a life of pain. His focus was not on acquiring the next pleasurable thing; his focus was on moving away from something inside of him that was deeply wounded.

And finally, there it was. I felt connected to him. I understood him. Because that's how I had spent most of my life. I was never focused on having good times in my life; I was focused on numbing the pain inside of me. I was never focused on making things happen to suit me; I was focused on trying to feel in control to counter that gnawing feeling deep down that I was never good enough. I saw that he and I had the same wiring. He is where I got my orchid genes from. I had unknowingly carried Dad within me every day of my life. Whereas before he was something wholly foreign and different, now he was internal and familiar. I am him, and he is me.

The difference is, I was able to find my way out of it. He wasn't. I'm pretty sure his death was, while not directly intentional, a result of him saying he was done trying to figure things out. He was tired of trying to escape the pain inside of him. He just decided to put his foot on the gas and let things happen.

It's a weird thing to be an addiction psychologist and have your father die from addiction. It's not an uncommon thing in my field. Counselors and other providers frequently have people they love die from substance use disorders. For a long time, I used to secretly judge these colleagues. *If there were better at what they do*, a quiet and critical voice would say inside of me, *that wouldn't have happened.* The rational part of me knew this simply wasn't true. I was projecting judgment onto others for not being able to do anything myself.

So now I am adjusting to this new relationship with Dad. I don't know how our relationship will evolve next, but I'm really interested in seeing what happens.

Healing 29

The Lucky Ones.

As I sit here today, reflecting on my life, I recognize I am one of the lucky ones. Yes, I spent decades in deep depression. I was miserable with mental health, eating and substance use disorders. I squandered years trying to survive by being invisible.

But I also recognize that this pain facilitated tremendous growth. All the peace and serenity I have today is a direct result of the misery I experienced for years. I don't get this without going through that. This is what *surthriving* is. I have been able to transform myself from a place of mere survival to one of truly thriving, in all the best ways. I have genuinely connected relationships—to myself, to my family, to friends, to my work. I experience all the best parts of being human, and I experience them deeply.

Because of my experience, and the experiences I've had working with clients with substance use disorders, I now believe that such people are incredibly special, incredibly lucky. We have been given lives with tremendous possibilities. Yes, those possibilities include the potential for a lot of struggle, strife, and toil. But we are also handed the rare opportunities for lives that are rich, deep, full of connection and a joy most people don't have access to. There is no need to pity us for having addiction or mental health issues. We just need a little help accessing the incredible parts of us.

A few years ago, my wife was dealing with a really difficult situation. She tried therapy, but it didn't really work for her. She's just not the type to deeply introspect. I remember thinking, *I am so lucky*. I could go to pretty much any corner of this Earth and have a built-in support system. All I had to do was look up the local 12-step group. AA alone has more than 115,000 groups in over 170 countries. There is no problem I can experience that won't find support there. I became aware of a feeling of sadness for my wife. She didn't have the same resources I did. Accompanying that sadness was a deep gratitude for all the help I had.

The truth is, I am the product of 26 years of public education, 20 years of 12-step recovery, a cumulative 12 years of therapy, four alcohol and drug treatments, and three eating disorder treatments. I found reprieve from my substance use disorder with the help of 12-step recovery. But 12-step recovery was not right for me to treat my eating disorder. I was able to overcome that with cognitive behavioral therapy. If someone had told me at the outset that all this is what it would take, I would have flipped them off and told them to go fuck themselves. And yet, now that I am on the other side, I see that no part of this experience was wasted. Every single thing I went through served a purpose and was necessary.

Knowing this allows me to approach clients' struggles with the mindset that somehow, everything they are going through is all necessary for them. I always hold a strong belief that there is a path through all their suffering where the person comes out on the other side happier and more whole. I often share this belief with new clients during their assessment. Clients are usually surprised when I say this. They have just spent an hour outlining how horrible things are for them, how broken they are. That I can come in after that and tell them not only will it be okay, but that they could be better than they can imagine, well, it just does something powerful.

It instills hope.

My journey has been long and difficult, but the reward has been amazing.

A Note to the Reader

I thank you for making it to the end of this book. This book is proudly independently published. The landscape of publishing has vastly changed over the past two decades, and it is now virtually impossible for a first-time author to get the help from a traditional publishing house. I pursued this route for two years with no success, receiving very little interest and all rejections, if I received any communication at all. I pivoted into independent publishing, which means I am the sole writer, publisher, and marketer for this book. I ultimately came to the conclusion that this was the correct route for this project.

However, because of this, the power of this success of this book now lies in the hands of the readers. Without the marketing support of a traditional publishing house, word-of-mouth and good reviews will be the driver of whether or not this book is a success.

To this end, if you found this book helpful, or at least interesting, I urge you to spread the word. I thank you for your support.

Acknowledgments

There are many, many people to thank for their support in this project. My wife, Sarah, my sisters, Mary Margaret Barker and Virginia Thomas, and my mother, Jorja Davenport, are first and foremost. This book certainly would not have happened without their support. I also want to thank numerous colleagues and friends for reading early drafts of the manuscript and providing valuable feedback: Amy Evans, Brenda Frye, Dede Armstrong, Tom Hegblom, Michael Schmit, Kevin Doyle, Jeremiah Gardner, and Samantha Moy-Gottfried. And I am forever grateful to count Steve Delisi as both a friend and a mentor; his enthusiastic support got me across the finish line.

I also want to give a special shout out to my editor, Jocelyn Carbonara, whose meticulous edits and suggestions brought this book into a whole new stratosphere. As a first-time author, I especially needed someone to provide a gentle path through the editing process, and she was just perfect for this job. I thank Joe Caravella for his help navigating the independent publishing process. I want to recognize the countless coworkers and students at the Hazelden Betty Ford Graduate School, whose words of encouragement kept this from being a lonely endeavor. I was buoyed, too, by numerous peers in recovery who helped me believe that I had something worth saying. And finally, a big thank you to the Hazelden Betty Ford Foundation for their support of this project.

Printed in Great Britain
by Amazon

45422394R00162